# 1791

The Massachusetts Historical Society is an independent research library that collects, preserves, makes accessible, and communicates manuscripts and other materials that promote the study of the history of Massachusetts and the nation—a mission it has pursued since 1791.

# COLLECTING HISTORY

Massachusetts Historical Society

Copyright 2009, Massachusetts Historical Society, Boston, Massachusetts.

ISBN: 0-934909-95-4
ISBN: 978-0-934909-95-2

Printed in the United States of America by
RR Donnelley, W.E. Andrews Plant, Bedford, Massachusetts 01730.

Designed by Jeffrey Williamson.

Photography of historical objects by John Holt, Dock 25, Boston, Massachusetts.

Cover:
Christian Remick. Perspective View of the Blockad[e] of Boston Harbour, circa 1768.
From the estate of Henry Lee Shattuck, 1970.

Inside front cover:
Thomas Jefferson. The Declaration of Independence. Manuscript copy, 1776.
Gift of Mr. and Mrs. Alexander C. Washburn, 1893.

DOCUMENTS IN INTRODUCTION:

Title page: Photograph of the Massachusetts Historical Society building, 1918.

Massachusetts Historical Society. Circular Letter, of the Historical Society,
1 November 1791. From the Massachusetts Historical Society Archives.

Paul Revere. Letter to Jeremy Belknap, Corresponding Secretary of the Massachusetts
Historical Society, 1 January 1798. From the Massachusetts Historical Society Archives.

CHAPTER HEADING DECORATIONS:

Chapter I
Signatures of John Adams, Thomas Jefferson, and John Quincy Adams.

Chapter II
Officer's small sword owned by John Thomas, anonymous European maker,
circa 1730-1740. From the estate of William A. Thomas, 1904.

Chapter III
Shem Drowne. Indian Archer Weathervane, circa 1716.
Gift of Emily Warren Appleton, 1876.

Chapter IV
John Singleton Copley. Untitled sketch of a rose, circa 1753.
Probably the gift of Frederic Amory, 1921.

Inside back cover:
James Brown Marston. State Street, 1801.
Purchased by subscription, 1879.

## CONTENTS

Acknowledgments   vii

Foreword by David McCullough   ix

Introduction   xi

The Personal Papers of Three Presidents   1

Politics & War   23

Mathematics & Philosophy, Navigation & Commerce   49

Painting, Poetry, & Architecture   67

# CIRCULAR LETTER,

## OF THE

## HISTORICAL SOCIETY.

SIR,

A SOCIETY has lately been instituted in this town, called the HISTORICAL SOCIETY; the professed design of which is, to collect, preserve and communicate, materials for a complete history of this country, and accounts of all valuable efforts of human ingenuity and industry, from the beginning of its settlement. In pursuance of this plan, they have already amassed a large quantity of books, pamphlets and manuscripts; and are still in search of more: A catalogue of which will be printed for the information of the public.

THEY have also given encouragement to the publication of a weekly paper, to be called THE AMERICAN APOLLO; in which will be given the result of their inquiries, into the natural, political and ecclesiastical history of this country. A proposal for the printing of this paper is here inclosed to you; and it is requested that you would promote subscriptions for it; and contribute to its value and importance, by attention to the articles annexed. The Society

beg

# Acknowledgments

Donors have made the Massachusetts Historical Society one of the greatest repositories of our nation's past. Few have holdings that can match the MHS in quality and significance. This publication celebrates the foresight, caring, and generosity of those individuals.

One especially generous donor, Peter Spang, needs to be recognized for his ongoing commitment and contributions to the Society. A trustee for many years, he has served as a vice president and the chair of the Collections Committee. His dedication to the Society exemplifies the tradition of giving that these pages illustrate. It is a very generous gift from Peter that has made publication of this compendium possible. He has our deepest gratitude.

We are indebted to David McCullough, a longtime friend of the MHS, for writing the foreword to this publication and supporting us in countless other ways. Peter Drummey, Stephen T. Riley Librarian, prepared the text, drawing on his encyclopedic knowledge of our collection. His cohort, Anne Bentley, our Curator of Art, added her expertise and project oversight. I also want to thank Brenda Lawson, Director of Collections Services; Mary Fabiszewski, Senior Cataloger; Nancy Heywood, Digital Projects Coordinator; Ondine Le Blanc, Director of Publications; Jeanine Rees, Assistant Editor; and Nicole Leonard, Associate Director of Development, for their contributions.

Well into its third century, the Massachusetts Historical Society takes this opportunity to share its riches with an ever widening audience and—we hope—a future generation of donors.

Dennis A. Fiori
*President*

Dear Sir,
Having a little leisure, I wish [to fulfil my]
promise of giving you some facts, & Anec[dotes of]
the Battle of Lexington, which I do not [see in]
any history of the American Revolution.

In the year 1773 I was imployed by the
Select[men] of Boston to carry the account of the De[struction of the]
Tea to New-York, & afterwards, 1774, to carry [intelligence to]
New-York & Philadelphia for calling a Congre[ss, after the]
Congress, several times. In the Fall of 1774 I was
one of upwards of thirty, chiefly mechanics, who formed [ourselves into a club]
for the purpose of watching the movements of [the British Soldiers]
& gaining every intelegence of the movements of [the Tories. We]
held our meetings, at the Green-Dragon [tavern. We were sworn]
our meetings should be kept secret; that every [member of this]
person swore upon the Bible, that they would not [reveal any of]
our transactions, But to Messrs. Hancock, Adams, Doc[tors Warren, Church,]
& one or two more. About November, when things [began to grow]
serious, a Gentleman who had connections with the [tory party,]
a Whig at heart, acquainted me, that our meetings w[ere known, and]
mentioned the identical words that were spoken amon[g us]
before. We did not then distrust Dr. Church, but [suspected]
some one among us. We removed to another pl[ace, which we]
thought was more secure; but here we found that all [our transactions]
were communicated to Govr. Gage. (This come [from Major]
then Lieut. Secretary Flucker; He told it to the Gentlemen mention[ed above). It was]
then a common opinion, that there was a Traytor in [the Con-]
gress, & that Gage was possessed of all their secrets. (Ch[urch was a member]
of that Congress for Boston.) In the Winter, towards the [Spring, we fre-]
quently took Turns, two & two, to watch the Soldiers [in]
the Streets, all night. The Saturday night preceeding the 19[th of April,]
about 12 o clock at Night, the Boats belonging to the Transpo[rts were all]
launched, & carried under the sterns of the men of W[ar. They had]
previously hauld up & repaired. We likewise foun[d]

# Foreword

There is simply nothing to compare to reading the original letters, diaries, and manuscripts of the American story, to hold the real thing in your own hands, the letters of John and Abigail Adams, for example, or of Thomas Jefferson. There is a tangible, tactile thrill one feels that no words can adequately describe. It is as close to those vanished people and their times as you can get, and the collections of such treasures at the Massachusetts Historical Society, all under one roof, are like none to be found anywhere else.

It would be hard for me to say which of those documents that I have worked with is my favorite. I love John Adams's famous letter to Abigail in which he so clearly understands the immense importance of the vote for independence cast on 2 July 1776 at the Continental Congress, but in which he also predicts the fanfare Independence Day will be given down the years, and foresees a vast continental nation besides. But then there are more than a thousand other letters between John and Abigail to choose from, and neither was capable of being dull or writing briefly.

As for the letters between Adams and Jefferson in their post-presidential years, they rank among the most remarkable in American history or, for that matter, in the English language. Still, I have to say the morning I first saw Paul Revere's own account of his historic night ride before Lexington and Concord was one I will never forget.

How wonderful that this handsome sampling of the full range of the treasures at hand has been provided now for so many to read and enjoy.

David McCullough

to be understood, would require more time and thought than I can possibly Spare. It is not indeed the fine Arts, which our Country requires. — the Usefull, the mechanic Arts, are those which We have occasion for in a young Country, as yet Simple and not far advanced in Luxury, altho perhaps much too far for her Age and Character.

I could fill volumes with Descriptions of Temples and Palaces, Paintings, Sculptures, Tapestry, Porcelaine, &c &c &c. — if I could have time. but I could not do this without neglecting my duty. — The Science of Government it is my Duty to study, more than all other Sciences: the Art of Legislation and Administration and Negotiation, ought to take Place, indeed to exclude in a manner all other Arts. — I must study Politicks and War that my Sons may have liberty to study Painting and Poetry Mathematicks and Philosophy. — My sons ought to study Mathematicks and Philosophy, Geography, natural History and Naval Architecture, navigation Commerce and Agriculture, in order to give their Children a right to study Painting, Poetry, Musick, Architecture, Statuary, Tapestry and Porcelaine.

Adieu.

# Introduction

The Massachusetts Historical Society holds more than 3,600 collections of personal and family papers—an unparalleled resource for the study of American history from the colonial period through the twentieth century. At the heart of its collections are the personal papers of three presidents, John and John Quincy Adams and Thomas Jefferson. Examples of their manuscripts, together with a letter from the irrepressible Abigail Adams, form the first section of this guide.

The remaining three sections are arranged according to the educational scheme that John Adams set out in a letter to Abigail in 1780. For the benefit of future generations, he wrote,

> *I must study Politicks and War that my Sons may have liberty to study Mathematicks and Philosophy. my Sons ought to study Mathematicks and Philosophy, Geography, natural History Naval Architecture, navigation, Commerce and Agriculture, in order to give their Children a right to study Painting Poetry Musick, Architecture, Statuary, Tapestry and Porcelaine.*

In the three sections that follow, "Politics & War" tells the political and military history of the United States through personal papers and artifacts. The second section, "Mathematics & Philosophy, Navigation & Commerce," covers the broad sweep of American social and business history. The final section, "Painting, Poetry, & Architecture," contains examples from the Society's art collection, as well as the writings and drawings of authors and artists.

John Adams. Letter to Abigail Adams, post 12 May 1780.
Gift of the Adams Manuscript Trust, 1956.

John

Th: Jeffe

John Qu

THE PERSONAL PAPERS OF
THREE PRESIDENTS

Miss Adorable

By the same Token that the Bearer hereof satt up with you last night I hereby order you to give him, as many kisses, and as many Hours of your Company after 9 O Clock as he shall please to Demand and and charge them to my Account: This Order, or Requisition call it which you will is in Consideration of a similar order Upon Aurelia for the like favour, and I presume I have good Right to draw upon you for the Kisses as I have given two or three Millions at least, when one has been rec'd, and of Consequence the Account between us is immensely in favour of yours

John Adams
octr 4th 1762

# John Adams ~ Letter to Abigail Adams
4 OCTOBER 1762   Gift of the Adams Manuscript Trust, 1956.

The courtship of John and Abigail Adams is chronicled by correspondence that began with a facetious contract written three years after they met. "Miss Adorable," her admiring lawyer addresses her,

> *By the same Token that the Bearer hereof satt up with you last night I hereby order you to give him, as many Kisses, and as many Hours of your Company after 9 O Clock as he shall please to Demand and charge them to my Account.*

The 1,200 letters exchanged by Abigail and John Adams form the cornerstone of the Adams Family Papers—the largest and most important manuscript collection held by the Historical Society.

Benjamin Blyth ~ John Adams and Abigail Adams, circa 1766.
Gift of John Adams, a great-great-grandson of the sitters, 1957.

# In CONGRESS, July 4, 1776.

# A DECLARATION
## BY THE REPRESENTATIVES OF THE
# UNITED STATES OF AMERICA,
## IN GENERAL CONGRESS ASSEMBLED.

WHEN in the Course of human Events, it becomes necessary for one People to dissolve the Political Bands which have connected them with another, and to assume among the Powers of the Earth, the separate and equal Station to which the Laws of Nature and of Nature's God entitle them, a decent Respect to the Opinions of Mankind requires that they should declare the causes which impel them to the Separation.

We hold these Truths to be self-evident, that all Men are created equal, that they are endowed by their Creator with certain unalienable Rights, that among these are Life, Liberty, and the Pursuit of Happiness---That to secure these Rights, Governments are instituted among Men, deriving their just Powers from the Consent of the Governed, that whenever any Form of Government becomes destructive of these Ends, it is the Right of the People to alter or to abolish it, and to institute new Government, laying its Foundation on such Principles, and organizing its Powers in such Form, as to them shall seem most likely to effect their Safety and Happiness. Prudence, indeed, will dictate that Governments long established should not be changed for light and transient Causes; and accordingly all Experience hath shewn, that Mankind are more disposed to suffer, while Evils are sufferable, than to right themselves by abolishing the Forms to which they are accustomed. But when a long Train of Abuses and Usurpations, pursuing invariably the same Object, evinces a Design to reduce them under absolute Despotism, it is their Right, it is their Duty, to throw off such Government, and to provide new Guards for their future Security. Such has been the patient Sufferance of these Colonies; and such is now the Necessity which constrains them to alter their former Systems of Government. The History of the present King of Great-Britain is a History of repeated Injuries and Usurpations, all having in direct Object the Establishment of an absolute Tyranny over these States. To prove this, let Facts be submitted to a candid World.

He has refused his Assent to Laws, the most wholesome and necessary for the public Good.

He has forbidden his Governors to pass Laws of immediate and pressing Importance, unless suspended in their Operation till his Assent should be obtained; and when so suspended, he has utterly neglected to attend to them.

He has refused to pass other Laws for the Accommodation of large Districts of People, unless those People would relinquish the Right of Representation in the Legislature, a Right inestimable to them, and formidable to Tyrants only.

He has called together Legislative Bodies at Places unusual, uncomfortable, and distant from the Depository of their public Records, for the sole Purpose of fatiguing them into Compliance with his Measures.

He has dissolved Representative Houses repeatedly, for opposing with manly Firmness his Invasions on the Rights of the People.

He has refused for a long Time, after such Dissolutions, to cause others to be elected; whereby the Legislative Powers, incapable of Annihilation, have returned to the People at large for their exercise; the State remaining in the mean time exposed to all the Dangers of Invasion from without, and Convulsions within.

He has endeavoured to prevent the Population of these States; for that Purpose obstructing the Laws for Naturalization of Foreigners; refusing to pass others to encourage their Migrations hither, and raising the Conditions of new Appropriations of Lands.

He has obstructed the Administration of Justice, by refusing his Assent to Laws for establishing Judiciary Powers.

He has made Judges dependent on his Will alone, for the Tenure of their Offices, and the Amount and Payment of their Salaries.

He has erected a Multitude of new Offices, and sent hither Swarms of Officers to harrass our People, and eat out their Substance.

He has kept among us, in Times of Peace, Standing Armies, without the consent of our Legislatures.

He has affected to render the Military independent of and superior to the Civil Power.

He has combined with others to subject us to a Jurisdiction foreign to our Constitution, and unacknowledged by our Laws; giving his Assent to their Acts of pretended Legislation:

For quartering large Bodies of Armed Troops among us:

For protecting them, by a mock Trial, from Punishment for any Murders which they should commit on the Inhabitants of these States:

For cutting off our Trade with all Parts of the World:

For imposing Taxes on us without our Consent:

For depriving us, in many Cases, of the Benefits of Trial by Jury:

For transporting us beyond Seas to be tried for pretended Offences:

For abolishing the free System of English Laws in a neighbouring Province, establishing therein an arbitrary Government, and enlarging its Boundaries, so as to render it at once an Example and fit Instrument for introducing the same absolute Rule into these Colonies:

For taking away our Charters, abolishing our most valuable Laws, and altering fundamentally the Forms of our Governments:

For suspending our own Legislatures, and declaring themselves invested with Power to legislate for us in all Cases whatsoever.

He has abdicated Government here, by declaring us out of his Protection and waging War against us.

He has plundered our Seas, ravaged our Coasts, burnt our Towns, and destroyed the Lives of our People.

He is, at this Time, transporting large Armies of foreign Mercenaries to compleat the Works of Death, Desolation, and Tyranny, already begun with circumstances of Cruelty and Perfidy, scarcely paralleled in the most barbarous Ages, and totally unworthy the Head of a civilized Nation.

He has constrained our fellow Citizens taken Captive on the high Seas to bear Arms against their Country, to become the Executioners of their Friends and Brethren, or to fall themselves by their Hands.

He has excited domestic Insurrections amongst us, and has endeavoured to bring on the Inhabitants of our Frontiers, the merciless Indian Savages, whose known Rule of Warfare, is an undistinguished Destruction, of all Ages, Sexes and Conditions.

In every stage of these Oppressions we have Petitioned for Redress in the most humble Terms: Our repeated Petitions have been answered only by repeated Injury. A Prince, whose Character is thus marked by every act which may define a Tyrant, is unfit to be the Ruler of a free People.

Nor have we been wanting in Attentions to our British Brethren. We have warned them from Time to Time of Attempts by their Legislature to extend an unwarrantable Jurisdiction over us. We have reminded them of the Circumstances of our Emigration and Settlement here. We have appealed to their native Justice and Magnanimity, and we have conjured them by the Ties of our common Kindred to disavow these Usurpations, which, would inevitably interrupt our Connections and Correspondence. They too have been deaf to the Voice of Justice and of Consanguinity. We must, therefore, acquiesce in the Necessity, which denounces our Separation, and hold them, as we hold the rest of Mankind, Enemies in War, in Peace, Friends.

We, therefore, the Representatives of the UNITED STATES OF AMERICA, in GENERAL CONGRESS, Assembled, appealing to the Supreme Judge of the World for the Rectitude of our Intentions, do, in the Name, and by Authority of the good People of these Colonies, solemnly Publish and Declare, That these United Colonies are, and of Right ought to be, FREE AND INDEPENDENT STATES; that they are absolved from all Allegiance to the British Crown, and that all political Connection between them and the State of Great-Britain, is and ought to be totally dissolved; and that as FREE AND INDEPENDENT STATES, they have full Power to levy War, conclude Peace, contract Alliances, establish Commerce, and to do all other Acts and Things which INDEPENDENT STATES may of right do. And for the support of this Declaration, with a firm Reliance on the Protection of divine Providence, we mutually pledge to each other our Lives, our Fortunes, and our sacred Honor.

*Signed by* ORDER *and in* BEHALF *of the* CONGRESS,

# JOHN HANCOCK, PRESIDENT.

ATTEST.
CHARLES THOMSON, SECRETARY.

PHILADELPHIA: PRINTED BY JOHN DUNLAP.

## The Declaration of Independence

1776   In the Historical Society collection before 1812.

The first printing of the document that founded the nation is the most important publication in the Historical Society collections. John Dunlap, a Philadelphia newspaper printer, turned out a small number of broadside copies on the night of 4–5 July, and independence was proclaimed in Philadelphia on 5 July 1776. On 18 July, Abigail Adams was in the crowd that heard the Declaration read aloud—perhaps from this very copy—from the balcony of the Old State House in Boston.

John Adams served with Thomas Jefferson, Benjamin Franklin, Roger Sherman, and Robert R. Livingston on the Committee of Five that the Continental Congress appointed to draft the Declaration. Jefferson prepared a rough draft that was revised by Adams and Franklin. Congress voted to adopt a resolution for independence on 2 July and continued to revise the Declaration until 4 July, when it authorized the Committee to print the corrected text.

In the documents that follow, the Declaration of Independence serves as a case study for the use of personal papers—letters and documents written by John and Abigail Adams and Thomas Jefferson—in the study of an epochal event in American history.

the House and furniture of the Solisiter General have fell a prey to their own mercileß party — surely the very fiends feel a reverential awe for virtue & patriotism, whilst they detest the parricide & traitor —

I feel very differently at the approach of Spring to what I did a month ago. We knew not then whether we could plant or sow with Safety, whether when we had toild we could reap the fruits of our own industry, whether we could rest in our own Cottages, or whether we should not be driven from the sea coasts to seek shelter in the wilderneß but now we feel as if we might sit under our own vine and eat the good of the land — I feel a gaieti de Cœur to which before I was a Stranger, I think the Sun looks brighter the Birds sing more melodiously & nature puts on a more chearfull countanance. we feel a temporary peace, & the poor fugitives are returning to their deserted habitations.

tho we felicitate ourselves, we sympathize with those who are trembling least the lot of Boston should be theirs. But they cannot be in similar circumstances unleß pusilanimity & cowardise should take poßeßion of them — They have time & warning given them to see the Evil & Shun it — I long to hear that you have declared an independancy — and by the way in the new Code of Laws which I suppose it will be necessary for you to make I desire you would Remember the Ladies, & be more generous & favourable to them than your ancestors. do not put such unlimited power into the hands of the Husbands. Remember all Men would be tyrants if they could. if perticuliar care & attention is not paid to the Laidies we are determined to foment a Rebelion, and will not hold ourselves bound by any Laws in which we have no voice, or Representation.

## Abigail Adams ~ Letter to John Adams
31 MARCH ~ 5 APRIL 1776   Gift of the Adams Manuscript Trust, 1956.

In the spring of 1776, with talk of independence in the air, Abigail Adams famously advised her husband,

> *I long to hear that you have declared an independancy —and by the way in the New Code of Laws which I suppose it will be necessary for you to make I desire you would Remember the Ladies, & be more Generous & favourable to them than your ancestors.*

Eliza Susan Quincy ~ Birthplaces of John Adams and John Quincy Adams, 1822. Gift of Eliza Susan Quincy, 1870.

A Declaration by the Representatives of the United States of America in General Congress assembled.

When in the course of human events it becomes necessary for one people to dissolve the political bands which have connected them with another, & to assume among the powers of the earth the separate & equal station, to which the laws of nature & of nature's god entitle them, a decent respect to the opinions of mankind requires that they should declare the causes which impel them to the separation.

We hold these truths to be self-evident: that all men are created equal; that they are endowed by their creator with inherent & inalienable rights; that these are life, liberty, & the pursuit of happiness: that to secure these rights, governments are instituted among men, deriving their just powers from the consent of the governed: that whenever any form of government becomes destructive of these ends, it is the right of the people to alter or to abolish it, & to institute new government, laying it's foundation on such principles, & organising it's powers in such form, as to them shall seem most likely to effect their safety and happiness. prudence indeed will dictate that governments long established should not be changed for light and transient causes: and accordingly all experience hath shewn that mankind are more disposed to suffer while evils are sufferable, than to right themselves by abolishing the forms to which they are accustomed. but when a long train of abuses & usurpations, begun at a distinguished period, & pursuing invariably the same object, evinces a design to reduce them under absolute despotism, it is their right, it is their duty, to throw off such government, & to provide new guards for their future security. such has been the patient sufferance of these colonies; and such is now the necessity which constrains them to expunge their former systems of government. the history of the present king of Great Britain is a history of unremitting injuries & usurpations, among which appears no solitary fact to contradict the uniform tenor of the rest, but all have in direct object the establishment of an absolute tyranny over these states. to prove this, let facts be submitted to a candid world for the truth of which we pledge a faith yet unsullied by falsehood.

He has refused his assent to laws the most wholesome and necessary for the public good:

he has forbidden his governors to pass laws of immediate & pressing importance, unless suspended in their operation till his assent should be obtained; and when so suspended, he has neglected utterly to attend to them.

# Thomas Jefferson ~ The Declaration of Independence

1776   Manuscript copy. Gift of Mr. and Mrs. Alexander C. Washburn, 1893.

Jefferson's draft of the Declaration was subjected to considerable Congressional revision. He was extremely unhappy with many of the changes and made several copies of the Declaration "as originally framed," including this one, to show his close friends how his text had been "mangled."

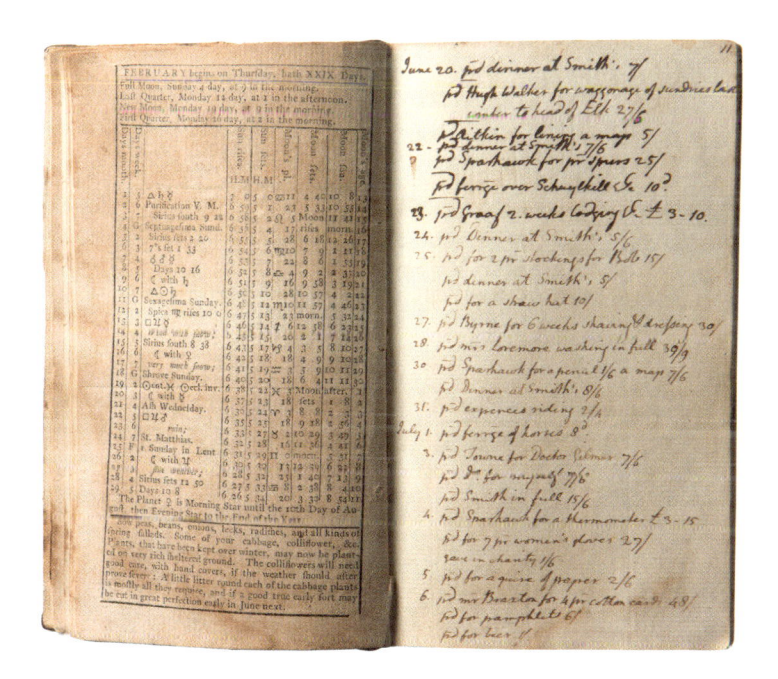

Thomas Jefferson ~ Memorandum book, 1776–1778.
Gift of Thomas Jefferson Coolidge, 1898.

Jefferson did not realize 4 July 1776 would become the "day of days." On that date, he recorded in his pocket account book shopping for a thermometer and gloves.

Philadelphia July 3d. 1776

Had a Declaration of Independency been made Seven Months ago, it would have been attended with many great and glorious Effects. — — — We might before this Hour, have formed Alliances with foreign States. — We should have mastered Quebec and been in Possession of Canada. — — — You will perhaps wonder, how such a Declaration would have influenced our Affairs, in Canada, but if I could write with Freedom I could easily convince you, that it would, and explain to you the manner how. — Many Gentlemen in high Stations and of great Influence have been duped, by the ministerial Bubble of Commissioners to treat. — — — and in real, sincere Expectation of this Event, which they fondly wished, they have been slow and languid, in promoting Measures for the Reduction of that Province. Others there are in the Colonies who really wished that our Enterprise in Canada would be defeated, that the Colonies might be brought into Danger and Distress between two Fires, and be thus induced to submit. — — Others, really wished to defeat the Expedition to Canada, lest the Conquest of it, should elevate the Minds of the People too much to hearken to those Terms of Reconciliation which they believed would be offered. These jarring Views, Wishes and Designs, occasioned an opposition to many Salutary Measures, which were proposed for the Support of that Expedition, and caused Obstructions, Embarrassments and studied Delays, which have finally, lost us the Province.

## John Adams ~ Letter to Abigail Adams
3 JULY 1776   Gift of the Adams Manuscript Trust, 1956.

John Adams seems to have understood more clearly than any other member of the Continental Congress the momentous importance of the vote for independence and how it would be celebrated by "succeeding Generations." He was right about everything except the date:

> *The Second Day of July 1776, will be the most memorable Epocha, in the History of America.— I am apt to believe that it will be celebrated, by succeeding Generations, as the great anniversary Festival. It ought to be commemorated, as the Day of Deliverance by Solemn Acts of Devotion to God Almighty. It ought to be Solemnized with Pomp and Parade with Shews, Games, Sports, Guns, Bells, Bonfires and Illuminations from one End of this Continent to the other from this Time forward forever more.*

All these Causes however in Conjunction would not have disappointed Us, if it had not been for a Misfortune, which could not be foreseen, and perhaps could not have been prevented, I mean the Prevalence of the Small Pox among our Troops. — This fatal Pestilence, compleated our Destruction. — It is a Frown of Providence upon Us, which we ought to lay to heart. —

But on the other Hand, the Delay of this Declaration to this time, has many great Advantages attending it. — The Hopes of Reconciliation, which were fondly entertained by Multitudes of honest and well meaning tho weak and mistaken People, have been gradually and at last totally extinguished. — Time has been given for the whole People, maturely to consider the great Question of Independance and to ripen their Judgment, dissipate their Fears and allure their Hopes, by discussing it in News Papers and Pamphletts, by debating it, in Assemblies, Conventions, Committees of Safety and Inspection in Town and County Meetings, as well as in private Conversations, so that the whole People in every Colony of the 13, have now adopted it, as their own Act. — This will cement the Union, and avoid those Heats and perhaps Convulsions which might have been occasioned, by such a Declaration Six Months ago. —

But the Day is past. — The Second Day of July 1776, will be the most memorable Epocha, in the History of America. —

I am apt to believe that it will be celebrated, by succeeding Generations, as the great anniversary Festival. It ought to be commemorated, as the Day of Deliverance by solemn Acts of Devotion to God Almighty. It ought to be solemnized with Pomp and Parade with shews, Games, Sports, Guns, Bells, Bonfires and Illuminations from one End of this Continent to the other from this Time forward forever more.

You will think me transported with Enthusiasm but I am not. — I am well aware of the Toil and Blood and Treasure, that it will cost Us to maintain this Declaration, and support and defend these States. — Yet through all the Gloom I can see the Rays of ravishing Light and Glory. I can see that the End is more than worth all the Means. And that Posterity will tryumph in that Days Transaction, even altho We should rue it, which I trust in God We shall not. —

Dear Sir                Monticello Mar. 25. 26.

My grandson Th:Jefferson Randolph, being on a visit to Boston, would think he had seen nothing were he to leave it without having seen you. altho' I truly sympathise with you in the trouble these interruptions give, yet I must ask for him permission to pay to you his personal respects. like other young people, he wishes to be able, in the winter nights of old age, to recount to those around him what he has heard and learnt of the Heroic age preceding his birth, and which of the Argonauts particularly he was in time to have seen. it was the lot of our early years to witness nothing but the dull monotony of Colonial subservience, and ~~of~~ of our riper ones to breast the labors and perils of working out of it. theirs are the Halcyon calms succeeding the storm which our Argosy had so stoutly weathered. gratify his ambition then by recieving his best bow, and my solicitude for your health by enabling him to bring me a favorable account of it. mine is but indifferent, but not so my friendship and respect for you.

Th:Jefferson

## Thomas Jefferson ~ Letter to John Adams
25 MARCH 1826   Gift of the Adams Manuscript Trust, 1956.

The story of the friendship of John Adams and Thomas Jefferson, completely broken in the aftermath of the bitter presidential election campaign of 1800, has a happy ending. Through the intervention of their mutual friend Dr. Benjamin Rush, Adams and Jefferson resumed their correspondence after a decade of silence. Over the next fourteen years (1812–1826), hundreds of letters flowed back and forth between Quincy and Monticello. In Thomas Jefferson's last letter to John Adams, he compares their roles in the Revolution to those of the Argonauts of Greek mythology: "It was the lot of our early years to witness nothing but the dull monotony of Colonial subservience, and of our riper ones to breast the labors and perils of working out of it."

While this letter from Jefferson to Adams is located in the Adams Family Papers, the Historical Society also holds an extraordinary collection of Jefferson's personal papers, the Coolidge Collection of Thomas Jefferson Manuscripts. The Coolidge Collection includes thousands of letters to Jefferson and copies of his replies, together with hundreds of his architectural drawings, the manuscript catalog of his library, and the farm and garden records of Monticello.

Maximilian Teich. 25. March 1829.

Louisa C. Adams.

John Q. Adams.

John Adams.

Mary L. Adams.

Mary C. Adams

Abigail S. Adams.

Mary Roberdeau.

# Jarvis F. Hanks ~
# The Family of John Quincy Adams
25 MARCH 1829   Gift of Richard Ames, 2002.

John Quincy Adams's single term as president was the unhappiest period of his long career in public service. Badly defeated in his bid for re-election in 1830, there was a brief hiatus in Adams's political career before he returned to office, serving as a member of Congress from 1830 until his death in 1848. Shortly after the Adams family left the White House for their home on Meridian Hill, John Quincy Adams noted in his diary,

> *Mr. Reynolds came with master Hankes who cut me out and all the family in paper. I had my wife and myself; my son John, his wife and their baby [Mary C. Adams and Mary L. Adams], Mary Roberdeau [daughter of family friend Isaac Roberdeau, of Philadelphia] and Abigail S. Adams [his niece, daughter of his brother, Thomas Boylston Adams], all cut out and pasted upon one Card.*

All are neatly labeled in John Quincy Adams's own hand.

The Frigate
of 10 6 Pound[ers]

The Horrid
of 8 6 Pounde[rs]

## John Quincy Adams ~ Illustrations from the end papers of volume 2 of his diary

1780   Gift of the Adams Manuscript Trust, 1956.

John Quincy Adams began to keep a diary when he sailed with his father to France in 1779, a diary that became over the course of sixty-eight years one of the most remarkable documents in American history—truly an American treasure.

*following pages*

## John Quincy Adams ~ Diary entry

29 MARCH 1841   Gift of the Adams Manuscript Trust, 1956.

In his seventy-fourth year, John Quincy Adams appeared before the United States Supreme Court to argue on behalf of Africans who had been kidnapped into slavery in Cuba but who had escaped to the United States by capturing the ship on which they were held, the *Amistad*.

Washington. Monday 29. March 1841.   Fire
29. IV: 30. Monday  } Rain the greater part of the last night and
Munroe E.              day, with a chilling east wind requiring a
                       fire in my chamber; just enough to be kept
Mr. Munroe was a stranger from Boston, who brought a travel for E
I completed the assortment and filing of my Letters received since
-ginning of this year, and find myself with a task before me perfectly
-ting — I am yet to revise for publication my argument in the case of
-tad Africans, and in merely glancing over the Parliamentary Slave
papers lent me by Mr. Fox, I find impulses of duty upon my own consc
which I cannot resist, while on the other hand, the magnitude, the dan
insurmountable burden of labour to be encountered in the undertak
touch upon the Slave-trade — No one else will undertake it — No one but a
unconquerable by Man Woman or Friend, can undertake it, but with
of Martyrdom — The world, the flesh, and all the devils in hell are arr
against any man, who now, in this North-American Union shall da
the standard of Almighty God, to put down the African Slave trade —
what can I, upon the verge of my Seventy-fourth birthday, with a she
hand, a darkening eye, a drowsy brain, and with all my faculties dr
from me, one by one, as the teeth are dropping from my head, one by
what can I do for the cause of God and Man? for the progress of huma
-cipation? for the suppression of the African Slave trade? — Yet my cons
presses me on — let me but die upon the breach — I walked about h
hour for exercise before dinner, and called at the house of Mr. S. St. F.
British Minister to have some conversation with him — It was 2. O'Clock
Servant at the door told me that he was not up, and that he was unw
enquired at what time he was usually visible — he said between 5. and
had heard that his usual hour of rising was 3. In my second walk after
I met Mr. Jesse D. Miller, first Auditor of the Treasury; from which Off
said he is to retire at the close of the present month and quarter. The se
I answered an old and repeated invitation to deliver a Lecture at Ri
Virginia; and postponed answering the Letters received last Evening
the Amistad Committee, and from Lewis Tappan — I read judge Betts
upon the 14th Section of the Tariff Act of July 1832. and the reversal of
cision by judge Thompson. And I made several minutes from the Par
-tary Slave trade papers Class A. 1839. 40. showing the enormous ext
which that trade was in those and the two preceding years carried o
American vessels under the patronage of N. P. Trist.

Washington Tuesday 30. March 1841.    Alexandria.

Tuesday.         Mr Charles Gordon heretofore an important clerk
Charles          in the General Land Office dismissed under the
Benjamin         Jackson administration for the colour of his political
Phineas          coat, afterwards employed three several times by
James Lloyd      direction of the Senate, as a draughtsman to protract
Walter           the Lands Surveys came to shew me a machine of his
James            own invention for protracting surveys made by the chain

pass. His dismission according to his statement was one of the first steps
 of confusion into which the whole management of the Office has
 extent of which may be imagined from the necessity of an act of Con-
 passed at the recent Session to legalize the whole mass of the
 tents issued for several years. Mr Gordon wants restoration to his
 Sumner came to set forth his equitable claims to a clerkship in one of
 ments here, consisting 1. In his wants. 2. In his misfortunes, having
 business as publisher of a compound newspaper in Boston 3. In the fact
 is not a single Bostonian in any of the subordinate public offices.
 ose is to be a Letter writer for sundry Newspapers, for which a Clerk-
 be a convenient location. He had a recommendation signed by
 ates and some others, but Mr Bates had neglected him, and it was said
 bers of the Massachusetts were not so zealous in supporting the appli-
 their constituents for office as others, but Mr Webster had advised him
 to Mr Ewing and Mr Granger, whose Departments had much more
 gethan his, but said that if he should fail with them, after all, he
 ke care of him. He promised to send me a copy of his address to the
 haritable Mechanic Association in 1836. Colº James Thomas was
 d gave me many details of the competitions for Office and for the
 l of Office some of which are humiliating. Walter Hallowell likewise
 w Hallowell and Mr Janney came with a carriage from Alexan-
 d took me down there, where I dined with Mr Edmund Jennings Lee
 rty of ten of his family and friends among whom were Majr Fowle,
 a Episcopalian Minister of the Church, his son Cassius Lee with his
 married daughter, besides Mrs Lee Hallowell, Janney and two or three
 after dinner, with most of the same company and some others, we took
 Benjamin Hallowell's - then at half past seven we went to the Lyceum
 I delivered my Lecture on Society and civilization to a crowded au-
 ter which there was a debate on the question whether phrenology is
 ce useful to the community. The meeting broke up between 10 and
 I returned with Mr Lee to lodge at his house.

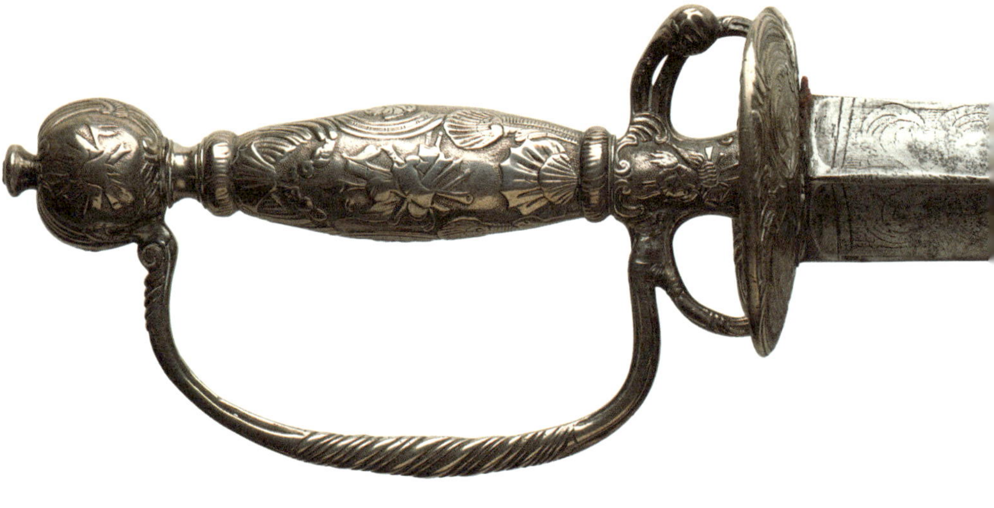

POLITICS & WAR

Beloved Sr:

I thanke you for your letter touching mrs Huchingson. I heard since of a monsterous, & prodigious birth which she should discover amongst you, as also that she should retracte her confession or aknowledgments of those errours, before she wente away; of which I have heard many various reports. If your leasure would permite, I should be much behoulden unto you, to sertifie me in a word or tow, of ye truth & forme of ye monster &c. Upon ye informatio & complainte of our neigbours at Sityate, I am requested by our Assistants to write unto you, touching a late partition, or limiting of confines betweene you & us; of which we heard noting till of late. Wherin we understande you have yntrenched farr upon those lands, which we have conceived to belong to us by right divers waies; as first by compossission, & compacte ancients with ye natives to whom ye right & sovrainitie of them did belonge, which did extend as farr as Conaqasete, which was ye bounds betweene ye Sachimos of ye Massa Thusets, & those of these parts; 2dly since late, been confirmed unto us by patents from his majesties authoritie. 3ly wheron we have possest it, & planted it some years agoe. We desire you will give us a reason of your proceedings eerein; as also that that ther may be a faire, & freindly desission of ye controuercie; that we may preserue peace & brotherly love amongst our selues, that have so many enimies abroad. Ther was not long since here with us mr Coltington & some oker of your people, who brought mr Williams with them, & prest us hard for a place at, or near Sowamos, the which we denit them; then mr Williams ynformed them of a seations yland called Monachunte, touching which I solisited our good will, to which we yoelded, (so they would compound with Osamequine) ye which we heard was yll taken by you, but you may please to understand yt it is not yn our patents (though we tould them not so) for yt only was excepted out of it. And we thought (yf they liked it) yt were better to have them, (though they differ in oppinions) then (easily) worse neigbours, both for us, & you. We thinke it is also better for us both to have some strength in ye bay. Thus comending you, & your affairs to ye Lord, with my love remembred to you selfe, & ye rest of my worthy friends with you, I take leaue & rest

Aprill. 11.
1638

your unworthy freind
William Bradford

# William Bradford ~ Letter to John Winthrop

11 APRIL 1638   Bequest of Robert C. Winthrop, Jr., 1905.

Governor William Bradford of Plymouth Colony writes to Governor John Winthrop of the Massachusetts Bay Colony about Anne Hutchinson ("Mrs. Huchinson"), who soon would be exiled from Massachusetts Bay in the aftermath of the Antinomian Controversy, and her supporter Mary Dyer, who would die as a martyr to religious freedom in 1660.

Winthrop family flint pouch with striking iron, 17th century.
Bequest of Clara Bowdoin Winthrop, 1969.

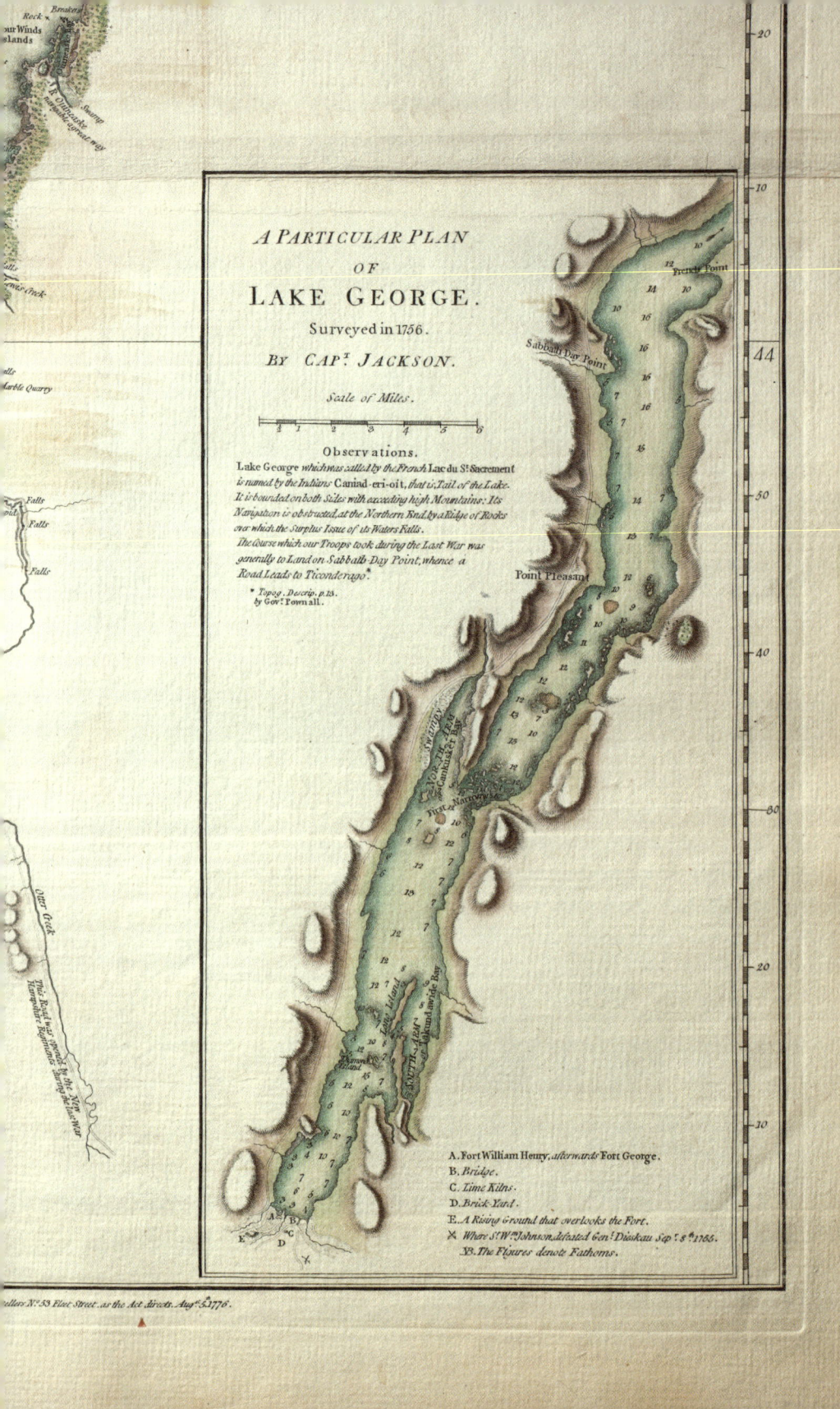

# A PARTICULAR PLAN
## OF
## LAKE GEORGE.
### Surveyed in 1756.
### BY CAPT. JACKSON.

Scale of Miles.

#### Observations.

Lake George which was called by the French Lac du St Sacrement is named by the Indians Caniad-eri-oit, that is, Tail of the Lake. It is bounded on both sides with exceeding high Mountains: Its Navigation is obstructed, at the Northern End, by a Ridge of Rocks over which the Surplus Issue of its Waters Falls.
The Course which our Troops took during the Last War was generally to Land on Sabbath-Day Point, whence a Road Leads to Ticonderago*.

*Topog. Descrip. p.13. by Govr Townall.

A. Fort William Henry, afterwards Fort George.
B. Bridge.
C. Lime Kilns.
D. Brick Yard.
E. A Rising Ground that overlooks the Fort.
✕ Where Sr Wm Johnson defeated Genl Dieskau Sepr 8th 1755.
N.B. The Figures denote Fathoms.

## William Brassier ~ Inset map of A Survey of Lake Champlain including Lake George

1776   From Atlas des Colonies Angloises en Amérique.
Gift of Count Jules de Menou, 1859.

The Lake Champlain–Lake George corridor was a prime invasion route for armies during the French and Indian War, the American Revolution, and the War of 1812. At the southern end of Lake Champlain a short portage connects to Lake George, which in turn connects via a twelve-mile portage to the Hudson River.

Head Quarters Newburgh
15th of March 1783.

Gentlemen,

By an anonymous summons, an attempt has been made to convene you together — how inconsistent with the rules of propriety! — how unmilitary! — and how subversive of all order and discipline. — let the good sense of the Army decide. —

In the moment of this summons, another anonymous production was sent into circulation; addressed more to the feelings & passions, than to the reason & judgment of the Army. — The Author of the piece, is entitled to much credit for the goodness of his Pen: — and I could wish he had as much credit for the rectitude of his Heart — for, as men see thro' different Optics, and are induced by the reflecting faculties of the Mind, to use different means to attain the same end; — the Author of the Address, should have had more charity, than to mark for

# George Washington ~ Newburgh Address
15 MARCH 1783   Gift of William A. Hayes, 1821.

At Newburgh, New York, during the waning days of the Revolution, George Washington confronted one of the greatest challenges to his command. The disgruntled officers of the Continental Army, long unpaid, threatened to force Congress to meet their demands. Washington's eloquent address to his officers recalled them to their duty and quelled their agitation before it became an open revolt. He appealed to both their military honor and their sentimental attachment to him. Having "grown gray" in their shared service, Washington found that he was "growing blind" and could not read his own handwritten address without stopping to put on his spectacles.

Pierre Simon Benjamin Duvivier, engraver ~ Washington before Boston medal, 1785–1789. Gift of Peter Harvey, 1874.

Congress awarded Washington this medal for his "wise and spirited conduct in the siege and acquisition of Boston."

WE the People of the States of New-Hampshire, Massachusetts, Rhode-Island and Providence Plantations, Connecticut, New-York, New-Jersey, Pennsylvania, Delaware, Maryland, Virginia, North-Carolina, South-Carolina, and Georgia, do ordain, declare and establish the following Constitution for the Government of Ourselves and our Posterity.

### ARTICLE I.

The stile of this Government shall be, " The United States of America."

### II.

The Government shall consist of supreme legislative, executive and judicial powers.

### III.

The legislative power shall be vested in a Congress, to consist of two separate and distinct bodies of men, a House of Representatives, and a Senate; ~~each of which shall, in all cases, have a negative on the other.~~ The Legislature shall meet on the first Monday in December ~~in every year~~.

### IV.

Sect. 1. The Members of the House of Representatives shall be chosen every second year, by the people of the several States comprehended within this Union. The qualifications of the electors shall be the same, from time to time, as those of the electors in the several States, of the most numerous branch of their own legislatures.

Sect. 2. Every Member of the House of Representatives shall be of the age of twenty-five years at least; shall have been a citizen in the United States for at least ~~three~~ years before his election, and shall be, at the time of his election, ~~a resident~~ of the State in which he shall be chosen.

Sect. 3. The House of Representatives shall, at its first formation, and until the number of citizens and inhabitants shall be taken in the manner herein after described, consist of sixty-five Members, of whom three shall be chosen in New-Hampshire, eight in Massachusetts, one in Rhode-Island and Providence Plantations, five in Connecticut, six in New-York, four in New-Jersey, eight in Pennsylvania, one in Delaware, six in Maryland, ten in Virginia, five in North-Carolina, five in South-Carolina, and three in Georgia.

Sect. 4. As the proportions of numbers in the different States will alter from time to time; as some of the States may hereafter be divided; as others may be enlarged by addition of territory; as two or more States may be united; as new States will be erected within the limits of the United States, the Legislature shall, in each of these cases, regulate the number of representatives by the number of inhabitants, according to the ~~provisions herein after~~ made, at the rate of one for every forty thousand.

Sect. 5. All bills for raising or appropriating money, and for fixing the salaries of the officers of government, shall originate in the House of Representatives, and shall not be altered or amended by the Senate. No money shall be drawn from the public Treasury, but in pursuance of appropriations that shall originate in the House of Representatives.

Sect. 6. The House of Representatives shall have the sole power of impeachment. It shall choose its Speaker and other officers.

Sect. 7. Vacancies in the House of Representatives shall be supplied by writs of election from the executive authority of the State, in the representation from which they shall happen.

### V.

## United States Constitution
6 AUGUST 1787   Gift of James T. Austin, 1829.

Elbridge Gerry's annotated copy of the first printed draft of the United States Constitution shows the evolution of the text as it was amended during the debates in the Philadelphia Convention of 1787. Gerry, a delegate from Massachusetts and signer of the Declaration of Independence, followed the debates carefully but refused to sign the Constitution because it contained no Bill of Rights. He later served in Congress, was governor of Massachusetts, and was vice president of the United States at the time of his death in 1814.

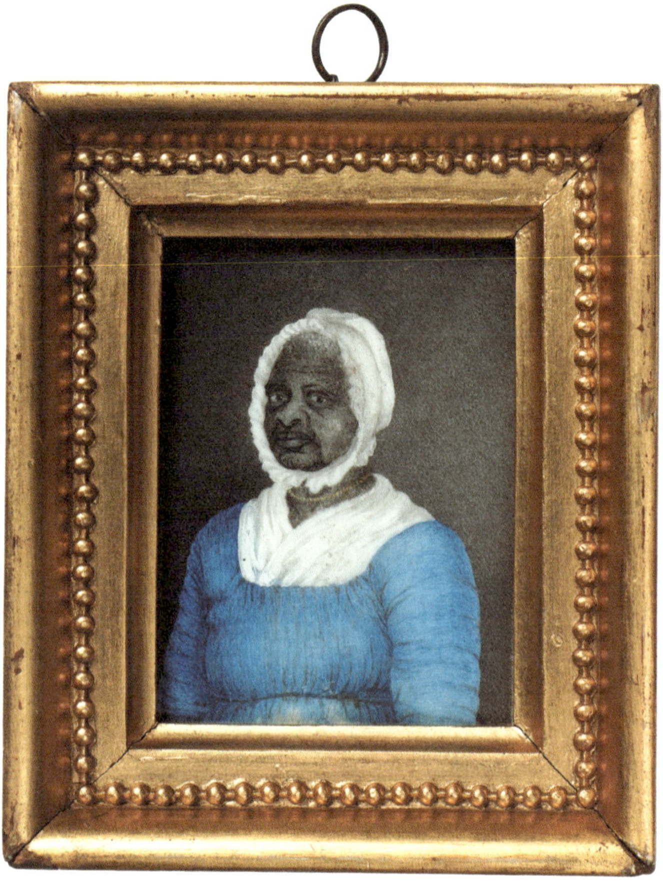

## Susan Anne Livingston Ridley Sedgwick ~ Portrait of Elizabeth Freeman

1811   Gift of Maria Banyer Sedgwick, 1884.

Elizabeth Freeman, familiarly known as "Mumbet," sued for her freedom from Colonel John Ashley of Sheffield, Massachusetts, in 1783, setting the legal precedent for the abolition of slavery in Massachusetts. She was represented by Theodore Sedgwick, who argued that Freeman should be freed under the Bill of Rights of the Massachusetts Constitution. It reads, "all men are born free and equal, and have certain natural, essential, and inalienable rights." Mumbet gave the necklace that she wears in this portrait to Theodore Sedgwick's daughter, the novelist Catharine Maria Sedgwick, who made them into a double strand bracelet.

Bracelet made from beads of a necklace worn by Elizabeth Freeman, circa 1840. Gift of William Minot, 1884.

# NO SLAVERY!

# FOURTH OF JULY!

## The Managers of the
## Mass. ANTI-SLAVERY SOC'Y

Invite, without distinction of party or sect, ALL who are ready and mean to be known as on LIBERTY'S side, in the great struggle which is now upon us, to meet in convention at the

## GROVE IN FRAMINGHAM,

On the approaching FOURTH OF JULY, there to pass the day in no idle glorying in our country's liberties, but in deep humiliation for her Disgrace and Shame, and in resolute purpose---God being our leader--- to rescue old Massachusetts at least from being bound forever to the car of Slavery.

## SPECIAL TRAINS

Will be run on that day, TO THE GROVE, from Boston, Worcester, and Milford, leaving each place at 9 25 A. M.

RETURNING---Leave the Grove about 5 1-2 P. M. FARE, by all these Trains, to the Grove and back,

## FIFTY CENTS.

The beauty of the Grove, and the completeness and excellence of its accommodations, are well known.

## EMINENT SPEAKERS,

From different quarters of the State, will be present.

Earle & Drew, Printers, 212 Main Street, Worcester.

## No Slavery ~ Fourth of July

1854  From the Historical Society broadside collection.

In 1854, the Massachusetts Anti-Slavery Society sponsored a Fourth of July rally in Framingham, where noted abolitionists including William Lloyd Garrison, Sojourner Truth, and Henry David Thoreau addressed the crowd. At the climax of the meeting, Garrison burned copies of the 1850 Fugitive Slave Law and the United States Constitution, proclaiming the Constitution "a covenant with death and an agreement with hell."

*following pages*

## The Branded Hand

1845  Albert S. Southworth and Josiah J. Hawes.
Gift of Nathaniel Bowditch, 1930.

In 1844, the letters "S.S."—for slave stealer—were branded on the right hand (the image is reversed in this early photograph) of Captain Jonathan Walker, a Cape Cod ship captain and ardent abolitionist who was arrested during a failed attempt to sail escaped slaves from Florida to the West Indies.

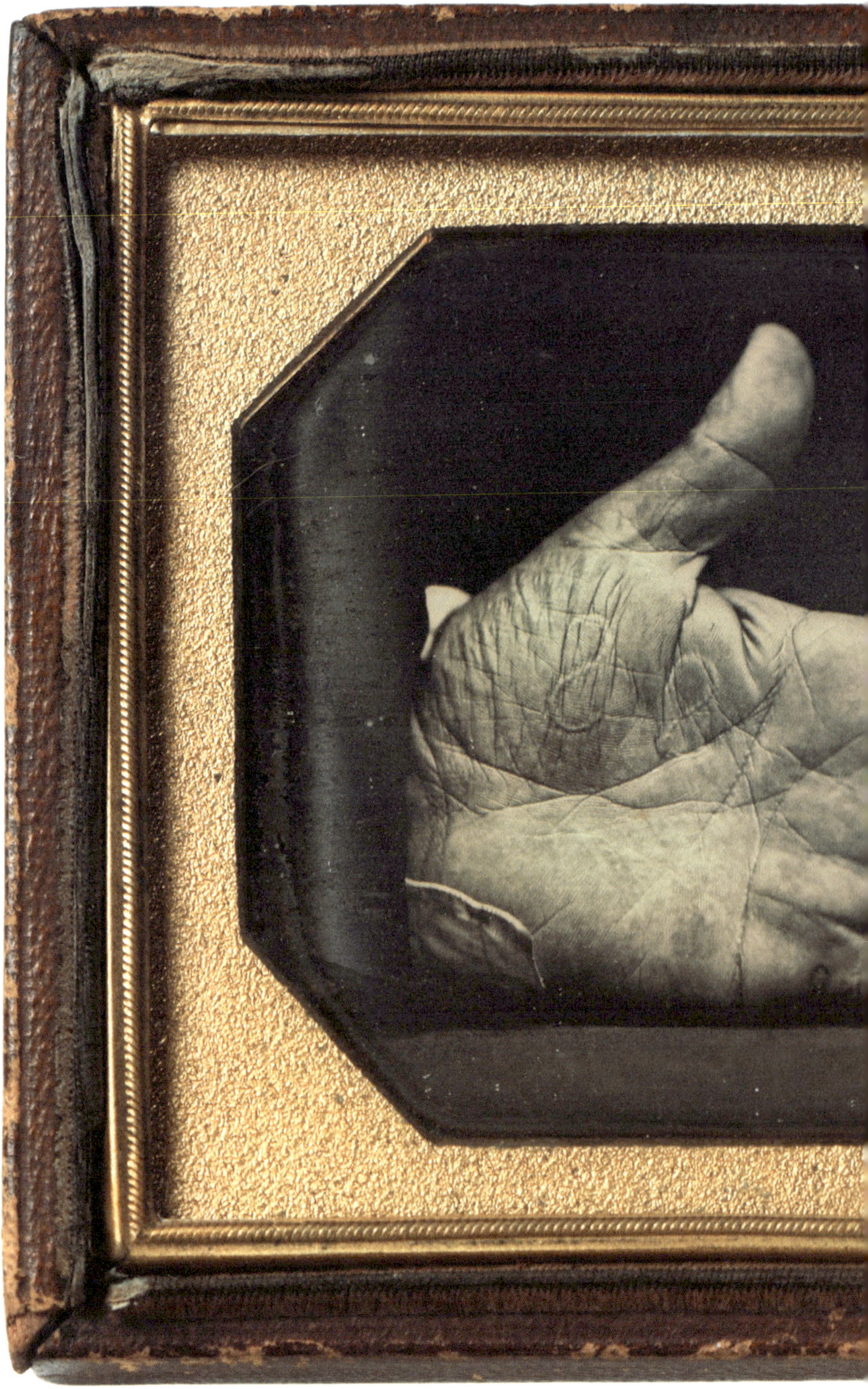

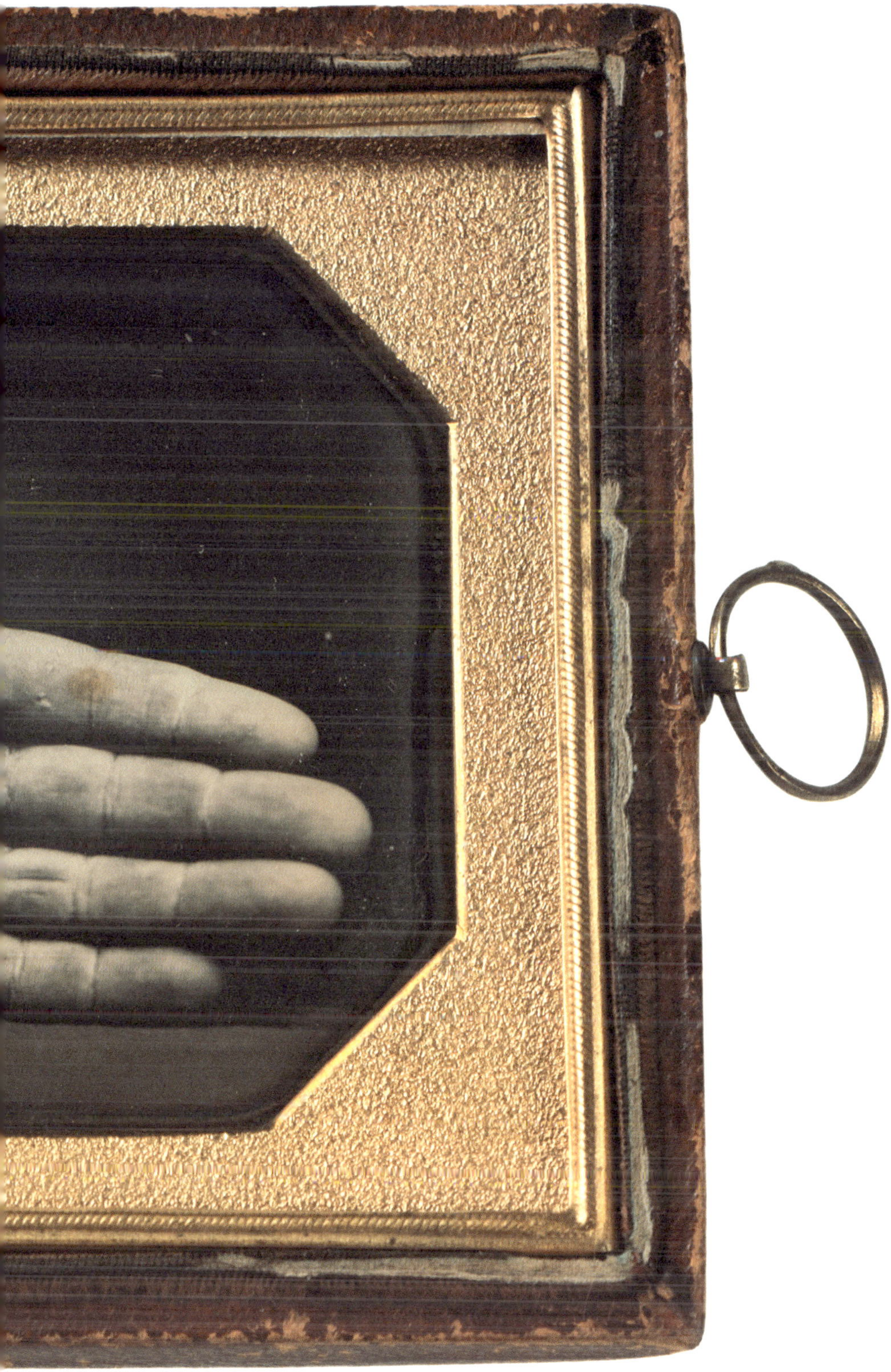

The President of the United States.

Rec. 21 Nov. 1863.

## Executive Mansion,

Washington, Nov. 20, 1863.

Hon. Edward Everett.

My dear Sir:

Your kind note of to-day is received. In our respective parts yesterday, you could not have been excused to make a short address, nor I a long one. I am pleased to know that, in your judgment, the little I did say was not entirely a failure. Of course I knew Mr. Everett would not fail; and yet, while the whole discourse was eminently satisfactory, and will be of great value, there were passages in it which transcended my expectation. The point made against the theory of the general government being only an agency, whose principals are the States, was new to me, and, as I think, is one of the best arguments for the national supremacy. The tribute to our noble women for their angel-ministering to the suffering soldiers, surpasses, in its way, as do the subjects of it, whatever has gone before—

Our sick boy, for whom you kindly inquire, we hope is past the worst.

Your Obt. Servt.
A. Lincoln

# Abraham Lincoln ~ Letter to Edward Everett
20 NOVEMBER 1863   Gift of the heirs of Edward Everett, 1930.

On 19 November 1863, the national cemetery was dedicated at Gettysburg. Edward Everett of Massachusetts, the greatest orator of the day, was the primary speaker. The next day, Everett and Lincoln exchanged letters concerning their respective roles in the ceremony. Everett wrote to Lincoln,

> *I should be glad, if I could flatter myself, that I came as near to the central idea of the occasion in two hours as you did in two minutes.*

Lincoln replied the same day,

> *In our respective parts yesterday, you could not have been excused to make a short address, nor I a long one. I am pleased to know that, in your judgment, the little I did say was not entirely a failure.*

Abraham Lincoln / Andrew Johnson presidential campaign token, 1864. Anonymous gift in the late 19th or early 20th century.

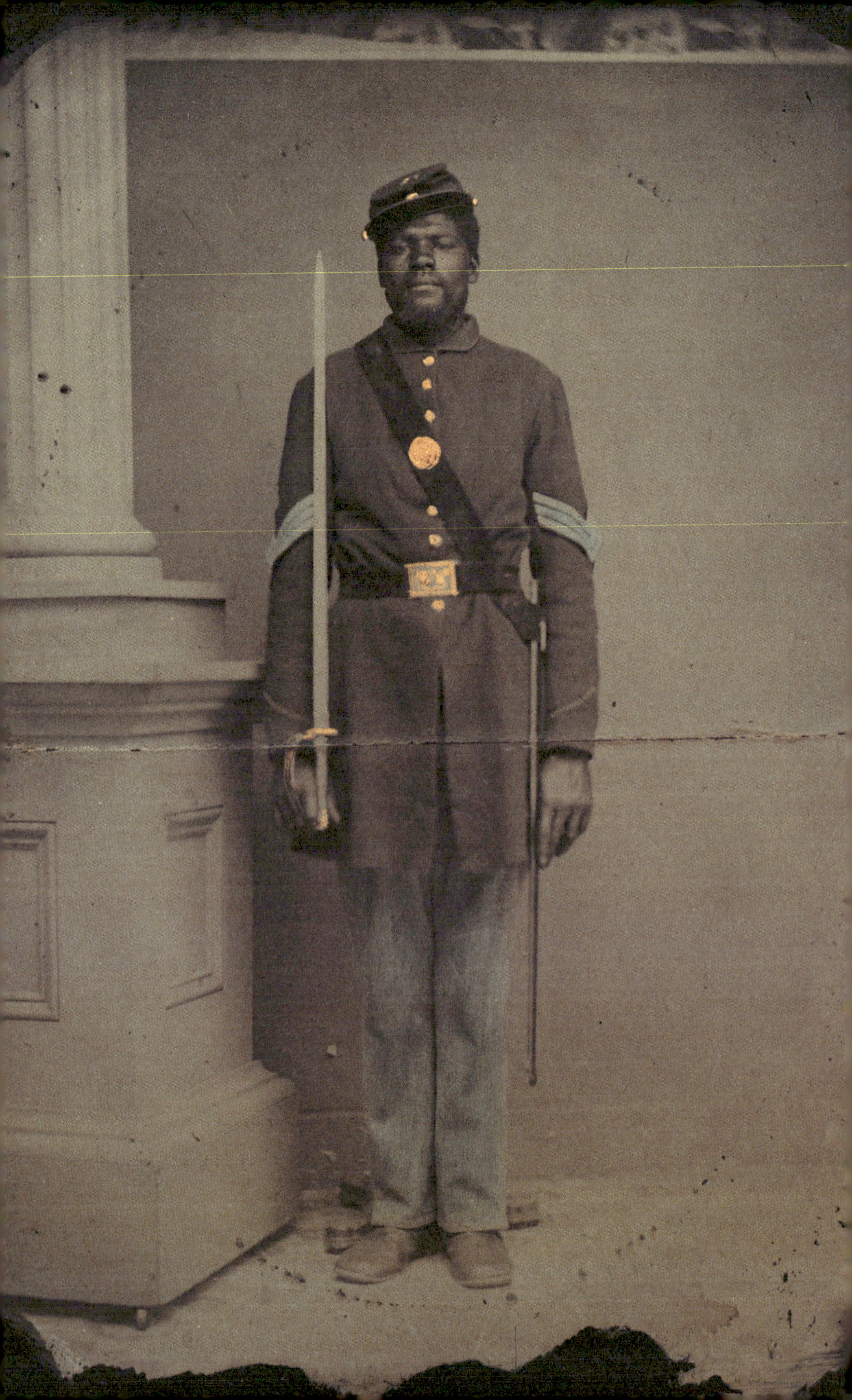

## Sergeant Henry Steward

1863   Unidentified photographer. Gift of Mary Silsbee Emilio, 1920.

After President Lincoln issued the Emancipation Proclamation in December 1862, Massachusetts was the first state to respond by enlisting African American soldiers. The Historical Society holds many manuscripts and photographs that document the service of Black soldiers and sailors in the Civil War. Highlights include those found in the personal papers of Governor John A. Andrew, who ordered the recruitment of the Massachusetts Fifty-Fourth Volunteer Infantry Regiment and offered the command to Robert Gould Shaw, as well as photographs and other materials collected for a history of the regiment by the commander of Company E, Captain Luis Fenollosa Emilio.

Sergeant Henry Steward (or Stewart) was a 23-year-old farmer from Adrian, Michigan, who enlisted in Emilio's company of the Fifty-Fourth Regiment on 4 April 1863. Steward died of disease at Morris Island, South Carolina, on 27 September of that year.

For God sake
have heavy       trenches outside
reinforcements        Santiago
sent us
instantly     July 3d 98

Dear Cabot;
            Tell the
President for Heavens
sake to send us
every regiment and
above all every battery
possible. We have
won so far, at a

[sideways:] cost of many lives with honor. We can't go back & we of our

## Theodore Roosevelt ~ Letter to Henry Cabot Lodge

3 JULY 1898   Gift of Henry Cabot Lodge, Jr., 1969.

> *Tell the President for Heavens sake to send us every regiment and above all every battery possible.*

Writing from the trenches outside of Santiago, Cuba, just after the Battle of San Juan Hill, Theodore Roosevelt thought that the campaign in Cuba—the event that was to make his political career—appeared to be on the verge of catastrophe. Within a few months of writing this letter, Roosevelt would be elected governor of New York.

Theodore Roosevelt in his Rough Rider uniform, 1898.
Photograph by Rockwood. Gift of Henry Cabot Lodge, Jr., 1969.

# Joan of Arc Saved France

Haskell Coffin

**W.S.S.** WAR SAVINGS STAMPS ISSUED BY THE UNITED STATES GOVERNMENT

## WOMEN OF AMERICA SAVE YOUR COUNTRY
### *Buy* WAR SAVINGS STAMPS
UNITED STATES TREASURY DEPARTMENT

### Haskell Coffin ~ Joan of Arc Saved France
1918   Gift of Henry Cabot Lodge, 1918.

More than 20,000 American women answered the call during the First World War, serving in the armed forces or as Red Cross and YWCA volunteers.

### Margaret Hall
11 NOVEMBER 1918   Photograph used to illustrate an entry in her Letters and Photographs from the Battle Country, 1918–1919. Gift of Emma L. Coleman, 1927.

Margaret Hall compiled a typescript narrative from letters and diary passages written while she was a member of the American Red Cross in France during World War I, and she copiously illustrated it with her own photographs.

THE WHITE HOUSE

WASHINGTON

August 5, 1963

Dear Senator Saltonstall:

    I am returning your letter from Mr. Bradley in which we are informed that there are some in Ireland who think you are my uncle. If you are ready to admit it, I am.

    With best wishes.

Sincerely,

The Honorable
   Leverett Saltonstall
      United States Senate
         Washington, D. C.

# John F. Kennedy ~ Letter to Leverett Saltonstall
**5 AUGUST 1963**  Gift of Leverett Saltonstall, 1967.

Senator Leverett Saltonstall heard through a friend, Ralph Bradley, that Philip Hofer, during a visit to Ireland in 1963, had been asked by a local man about the health of "That old Senator Saltonstall—him, that is uncle to Pres. Kennedy." Saltonstall sent the story on to the president, who replied, "we are informed that there are some in Ireland who think you are my uncle. If you are ready to admit it, I am."

John F. Kennedy and Leverett Saltonstall, by an unknown photographer, 1959. Gift of Leverett Saltonstall, 1967.

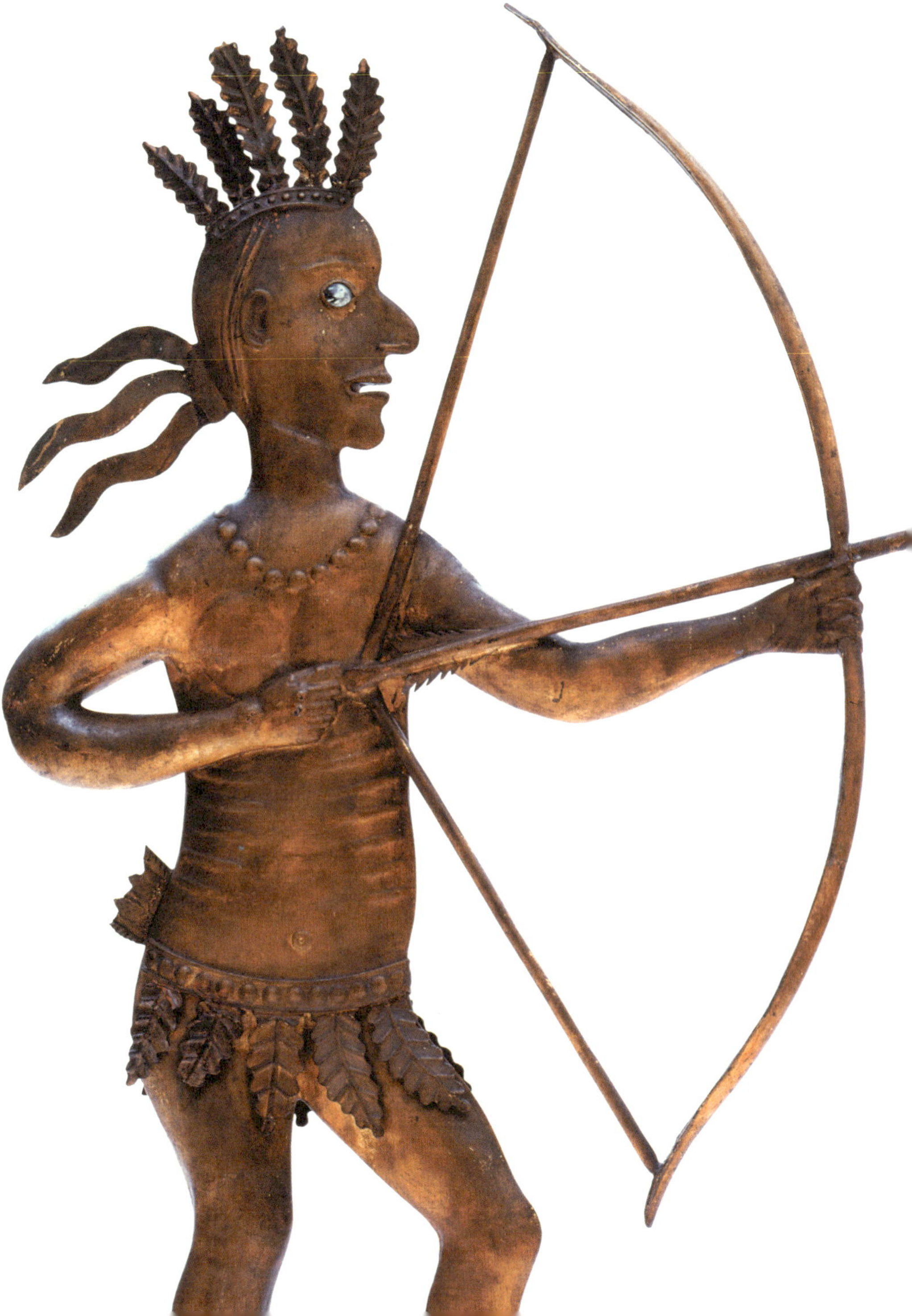

MATHEMATICS & PHILOSOPHY
NAVIGATION & COMMERCE

# MAMUSSE
## WUNNEETUPANATAMWE
# UP-BIBLUM GOD
## NANEESWE
# NUKKONE TESTAMENT
## KAH WONK
# WUSKU TESTAMENT.

Ne quoshkinnumuk nashpe Wuttinneumoh *CHRIST*
noh asoowesit

# JOHN ELIOT.

*CAMBRIDGE:*
Printeuoop nashpe *Samuel Green* kah *Marmaduke Johnson.*
1663.

## Mamusse Wunneetupanatamwe Up-Biblum God ~ The Eliot Indian Bible
1663   Gift of a Mrs. Coffin, 1793.

According to the Charter of the Massachusetts Bay Company, "the principall ende of this plantation . . . [is] to wyn and incite the natives of the country, to the knowledge and obedience of the onlie true God." Reverend John Eliot, the chief missionary agent in this effort, undertook to translate and publish the Bible in the Algonquin language spoken in eastern New England. The "Eliot Indian Bible" was the first large-scale printing project in Massachusetts. In the end, however, it was a tragic failure; most copies were destroyed in the turmoil of King Philip's War, which was, per capita, the most destructive war in American history.

*following pages*

## John Foster ~ A Map of New England
1677   Gift of Robert C. Winthrop, Jr., 1895.

The first map engraved and printed in British North America is attributed to John Foster, a mathematician and schoolmaster, who was the first printer in Boston. The map originally appeared in William Hubbard's *A Narrative of the Troubles with the Indians in New-England*, the best early account of the Indian Wars published in America.

There are more than 5,000 historical maps and charts in the Society's collections as well as early printed books illustrated with maps.

Newhaven
Gilford
Sey-brook
Mattabesick
Harford
Winsor
16
14
Northamton
13
12
Springfield
15 Hadly
Newlondon
Pequid Country
9
Sqabaog
Wajuset Hill
Stoniton
Nipmuk
17
Lancoster
21
Naraganset
31
Malborough
23
Groton
Sudbury
19
8
32
Water-town
33
Concord
18
Medfield
28
Dedā
25
Cambridg
39
Woburn
20
Providen
Roxbury
Newport
RHODE ISLAND
Mount-hope
1
2
Seaconk
Dorchester
Boston
Brantry
Lyn
Salē
Weymoth
Hingam
Marblehead
Pocasset 6
7
Taunton
Plimouth
4
3
Situat
Hul
Sandwic
Martins Vineyard
Yarmoth
Cape Cod
Nantuket

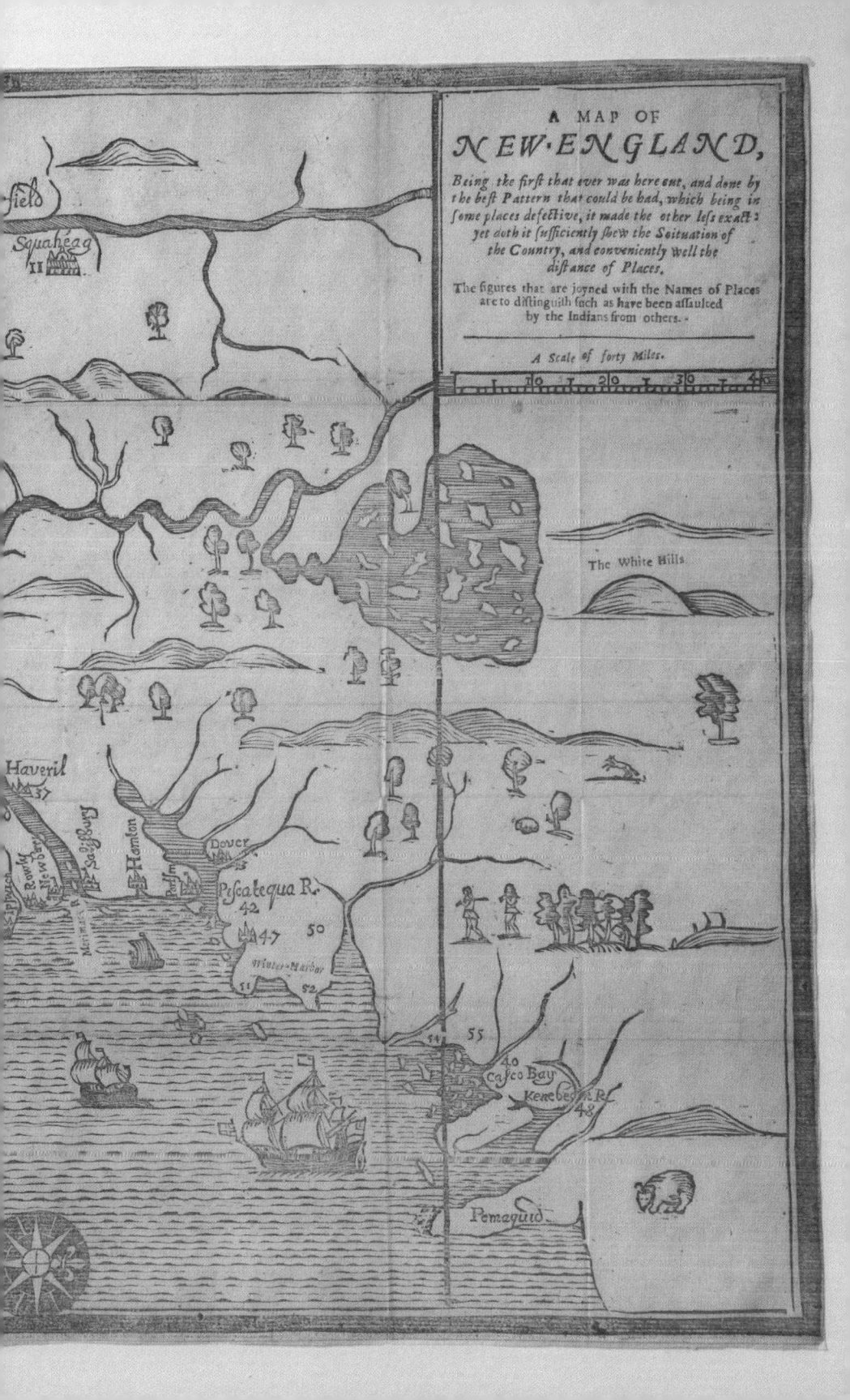

## A MAP OF NEW-ENGLAND,

*Being the first that ever was here cut, and done by the best Pattern that could be had, which being in some places defective, it made the other less exact: yet doth it sufficiently shew the Scituation of the Country, and conveniently well the distance of Places.*

*The figures that are joyned with the Names of Places are to distinguish such as have been assaulted by the Indians from others.*

A Scale of forty Miles.

The White Hills.

Squaheag

Haveril 37
Rowly
Newbery
Merimak R.
Salsbury
Hamton
Exiton
Dover 13
Piscatequa R. 42
47  50
Winter-Harbor
51  52
55
40 Casco Bay
Kenebeck R. 48
Pemaquid

These may certify, that
_Israel Keith Esq._ has diligently
attended an entire course of my
Anatomical Lectures & Demonstrations; to-
-gether with Physiological & Surgical obser-
-vations, at the dissecting Theatre in the
American Hospital, Boston: whereby
he has had an opportunity of acquiring
an accurate knowledge in the structure
of the human body.    _John Warren F.M.S._

BOSTON
March 1st
1782.

## Paul Revere ~ Engraver

28 MARCH 1782   Certificate of attendance at Dr. Warren's course of anatomical lectures. Completed in manuscript by John Warren. Gift of Dr. J. Collins Warren, 1921.

Dr. John Warren was the younger brother of Dr. Joseph Warren, the patriot leader who was killed at the Battle of Bunker Hill. During the Revolution, John Warren was the medical director of the military hospital in Boston where he began his anatomical lectures in 1780. He later was a founder of the Harvard Medical School and the Boston Medical Society. The Historical Society's collection of the personal papers of physicians includes four generations of the Warren family.

*following pages*

## Harvard Hall

CIRCA 1700–1750   Embroidery attributed to Mary Leverett Denison Rogers. Given circa 1795.

Samuel Eliot Morison attributed this early embroidered view of Harvard Hall at Harvard College to Mary Leverett, the daughter and granddaughter of Harvard presidents. The Latin motto found on the embroidery is from Virgil. It reads, "They keep out drones from these premises."

The Historical Society holds important collections for the history of education in Massachusetts and has published *Biographical Sketches of Graduates of Harvard University* ("Sibley's Harvard Graduates") since 1873.

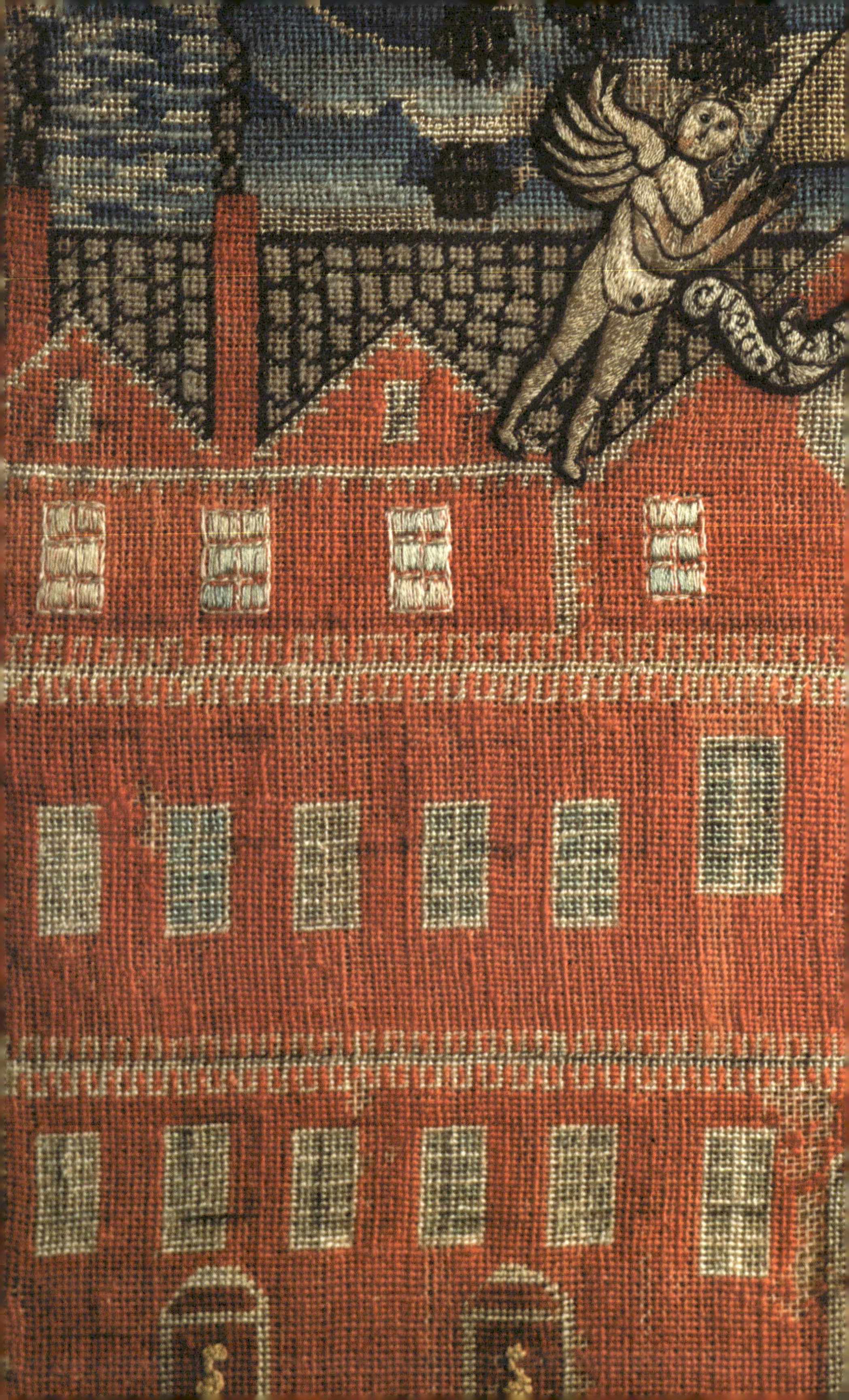

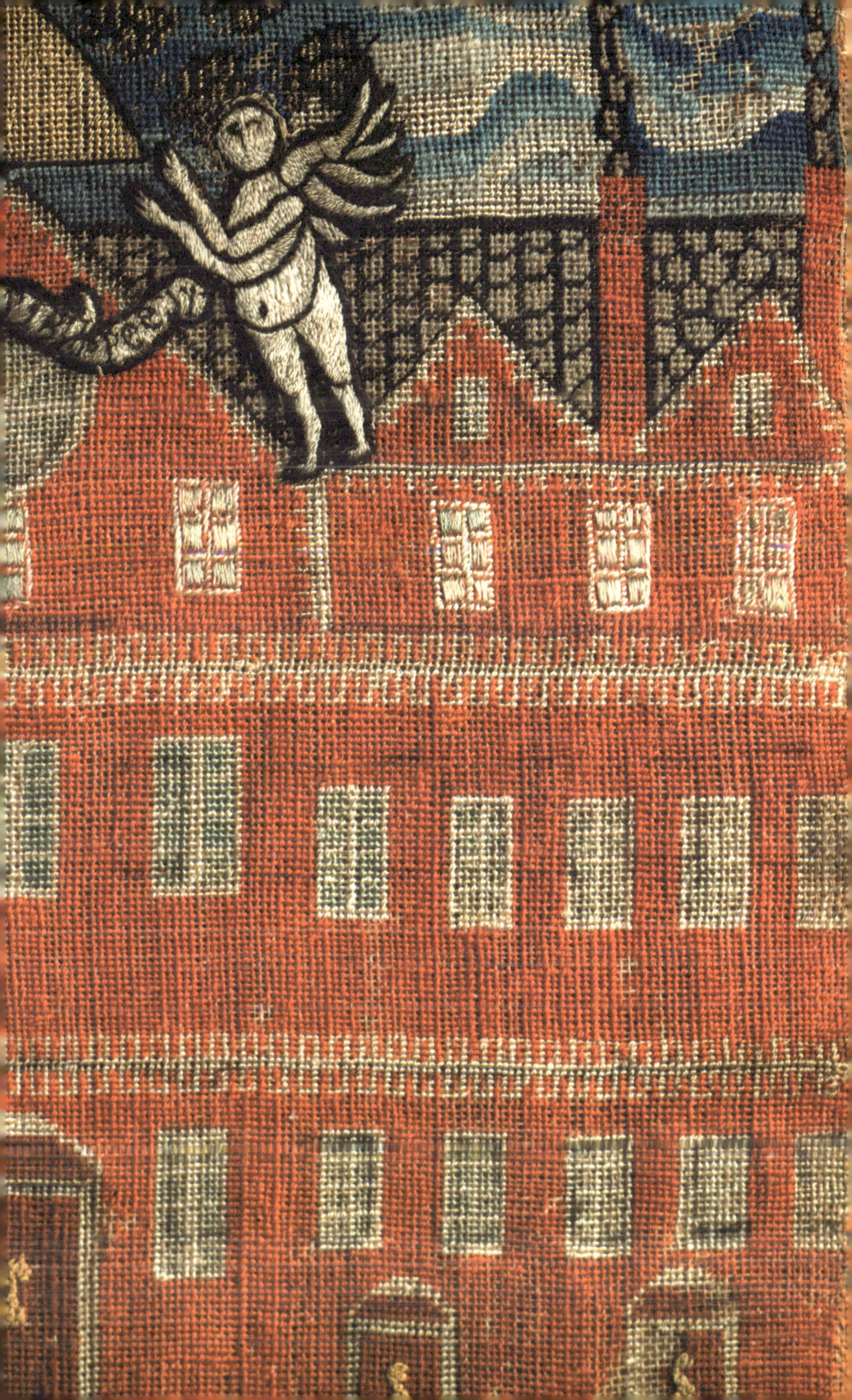

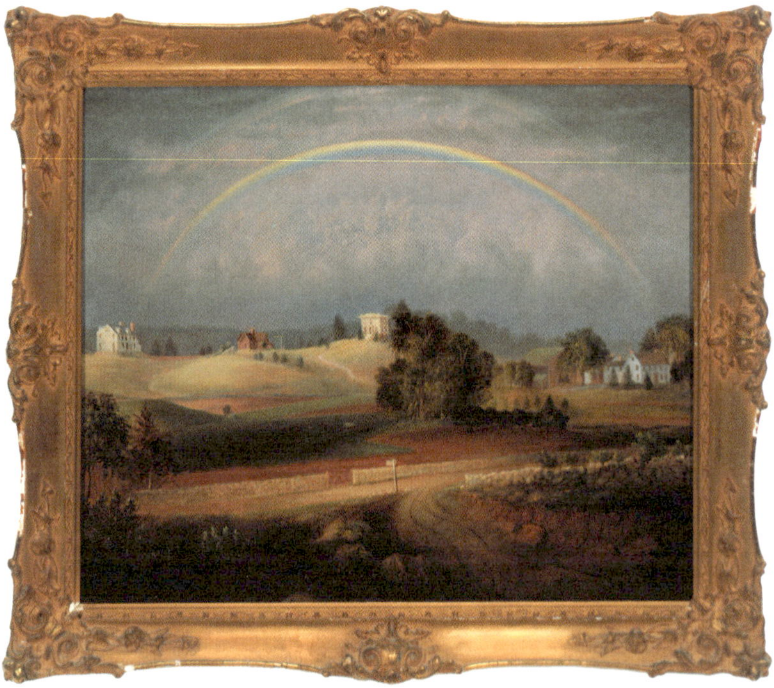

# Josiah Wolcott ~ Brook Farm with Rainbow
CIRCA 1845   Gift of Mrs. Robert B. Watson, 2005.

In 1841, George and Sophia Ripley founded the Brook Farm Institute of Agriculture and Education, the best-known utopian experiment in America, in West Roxbury, Massachusetts. They envisioned the cooperative community as a social application of Transcendentalism. To support their experiment in "plain living and high thinking," the Brook Farmers ran a progressive school; published a journal devoted to social reform, *The Harbinger;* and manufactured oil lamps and other utilitarian pewter ware. In addition to the manuscripts of participants, the Historical Society holds two contemporary views of Brook Farm painted by Josiah Wolcott, who was a member of the community.

Pewter oil lamp attributed to Ephraim Capen, Brook Farm, circa 1845–1847. Gift of Ron Bourgeault, 2006.

COLUMBIA AND WASHINGTON
COMMANDED BY J.KENDRICK

FITTED AT BOSTON N.AMERICA FOR THE PACIFIC OCEAN
BY
J·BARRELL.
S·BROWN, C·BULFINCH.
J·DARBY, C·HATCH.
J·M·PINTARD.
1787.

## The Voyage of the Columbia

At the close of the Revolution, New England merchants were eager to trade with the East Indies and with Canton, China, in particular. The ship *Columbia-Rediviva* and the sloop *Lady Washington* opened the Boston–China Trade by sailing around Cape Horn to the Northwest coast (hence the name of the Columbia River) where they traded for sea otter furs, highly prized in China; on to the Hawaiian Islands for sandalwood; and then to Canton. During the course of the voyage, the crews of the *Columbia* and *Lady Washington* distributed copies of a medal struck to commemorate the "adventure on the Pacific Ocean." The sponsors also sent a copy to the recently founded Massachusetts Historical Society. When the *Columbia* returned to Boston by sailing across the Indian Ocean and around the Cape of Good Hope, it was the first American ship to circumnavigate the globe.

## Columbia and Washington Medal

1797   Gift of Joseph Barrell on behalf of the merchants who sponsored that voyage.

*following pages*

## Robert Haswell

1787–1789   A Voyage Round the World Onboard the Ship Columbia-Rediviva and Sloop Washington. Gift of Rebecca Haswell Clarke Cummings, 1947.

# A VOYAGE

## ROUND THE WORLD
### ONBOARD THE SHIP
# COLUMBIA-REDIVIVA
### and Sloop
# WASHINGTON.

# A VOYAGE
# ROUND THE WORLD

*Early* in the fitting of the Columbia 1787 Sept.
for a Voyage round the World: I was employed
as Third Officer; Great expedition was used
to forward our departure and on the
the Ship was hauled off from the wharf and
anchored in the Harbour; here numberless
articles of her provisions stores &c.ª were received
onboard and on the       the Pilot came onboard
and we were removed down to the Castle roads
where we anchored with the small bower and
moored with the stream anchor.

    Friday the       the Sloop Washington
Captain Rob.t Gray. who is to be our con=
=sert; anchored in the Roads.

    Saturday y.e       I took my Baggage
onboard and in the afternoon. M.r D. Ingraham
the second Mate came onboard with his
baggage &c.ª for the first time: till late
in the evening all hands were employed
          (clearing)

TO
Made by
Capt. GAMALIEL BRADFORD
in the Streights of Gibraltar
This URN is Presented to him

## Paul Revere ~ Urn

CIRCA 1800   Gift of Helen Ford Bradford and Sarah Bradford Ross, 1933. Photograph © 2009 Museum of Fine Arts, Boston.

> To Perpetuate *The Gallant defence* Made by Captain Gamaliel Bradford *in the Ship Industry* on the 8th of July 1800.

Gamaliel Bradford received this silver urn for his role in a dramatic action against French privateers in the Mediterranean during the undeclared war between the United States and revolutionary France. A veteran of the American Revolution, Bradford was an early member of the Historical Society. He lost a leg in the fight with the privateers but later returned to sea before retiring to become the warden of the Massachusetts State Prison.

After the Revolution, Paul Revere continued to work as a gold- and silversmith, designing pieces in the neoclassical style, but the Revere family business papers show him to be also a technological innovator and business entrepreneur. In his workshops in Boston and Canton, Massachusetts, he began to produce copper fittings for ships and buildings and cast bells and cannon.

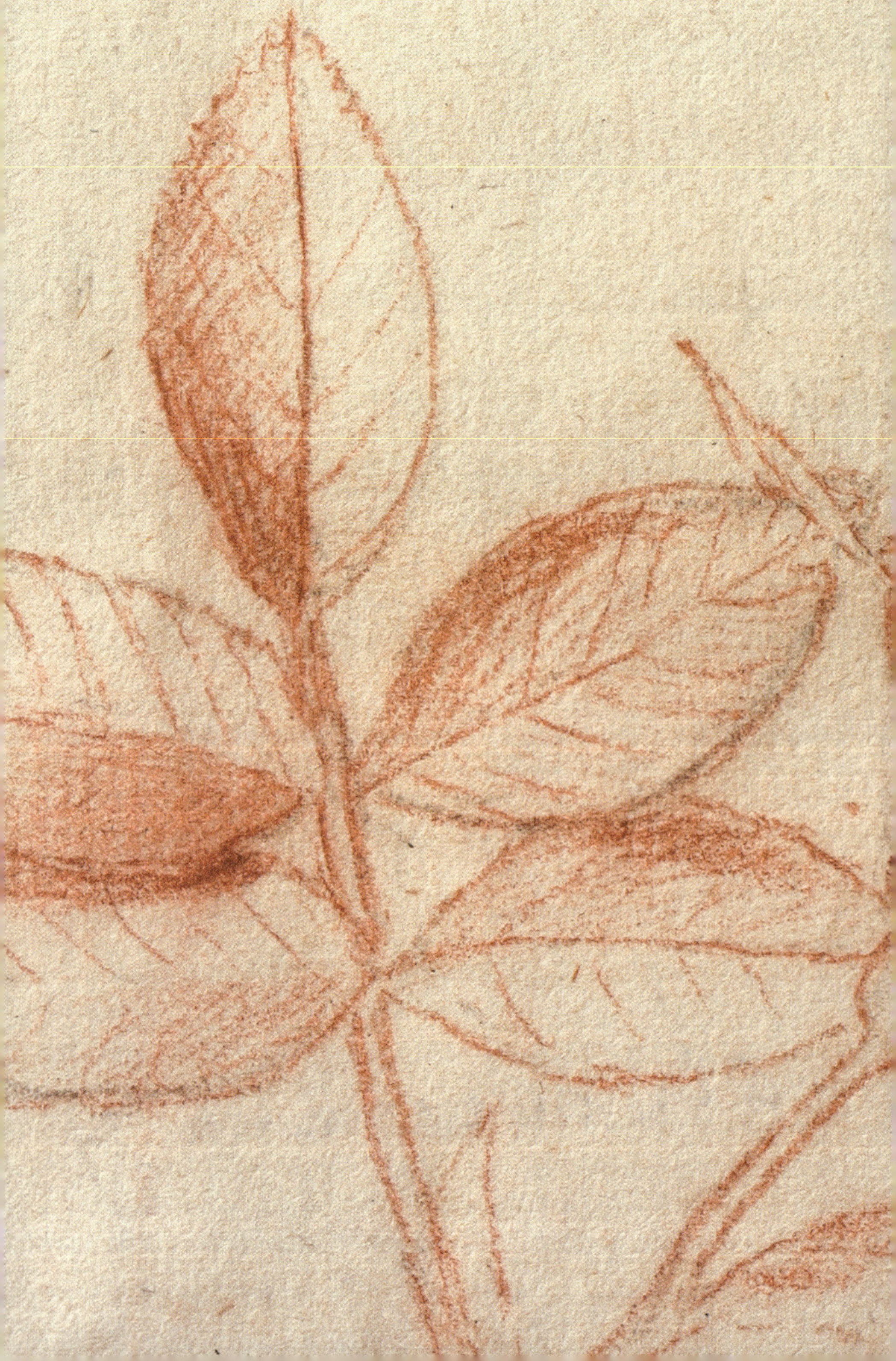

PAINTING, POETRY, & ARCHITECTURE

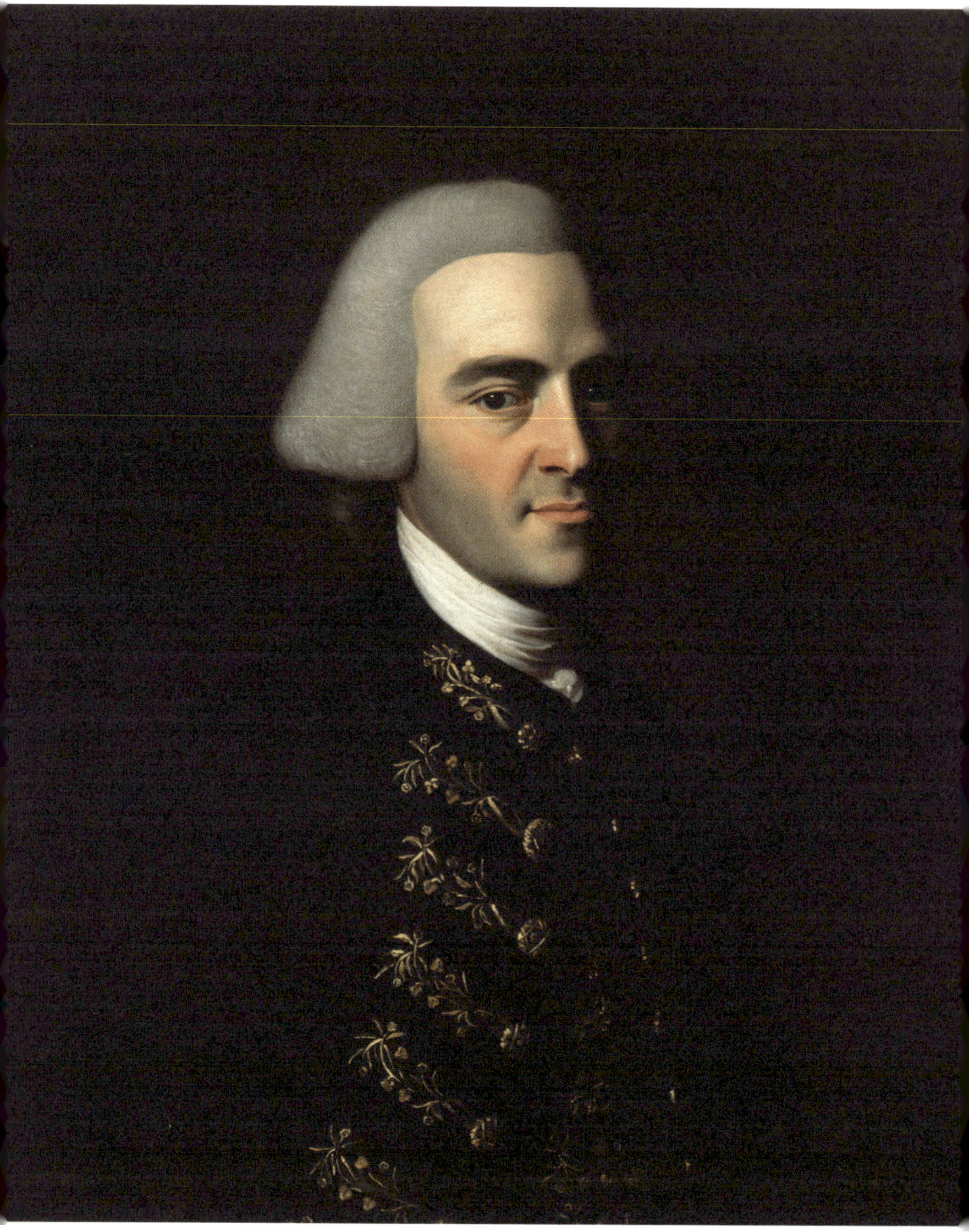

## John Singleton Copley ~ Portrait of John Hancock
CIRCA 1770–1772   Bequest of Henry Lee Shattuck, 1971.

John Singleton Copley learned to paint and engrave in the shop of his stepfather, Henry Pelham. Between 1753, the year of Copley's first works, and 1774, the year he left America for London, he became eighteenth-century Boston's preeminent portrait painter. Copley painted this portrait of Hancock soon after the 1768 seizure of one of his ships, the *Liberty*. The riot that followed transformed the wealthy Boston merchant into a patriotic victim of English oppression.

Though portraits were not on its stated lists of preferred collections in its early circular letters, the Historical Society stressed its desire to be of "public utility," promising to "plant a forest, into which every inquirer may enter at his pleasure, and find something adapted to his purpose." The first portrait added to the collections was an anonymous "head" of Governor Thomas Hutchinson, traded for a collection of seashells in 1796. The Society now holds more than 340 portraits that form a colorful adjunct to the core collections of personal and family papers.

Gold knee buckles of John Hancock attributed to Joseph Richardson, Jr., of Philadelphia, circa 1780. Provenance unknown.

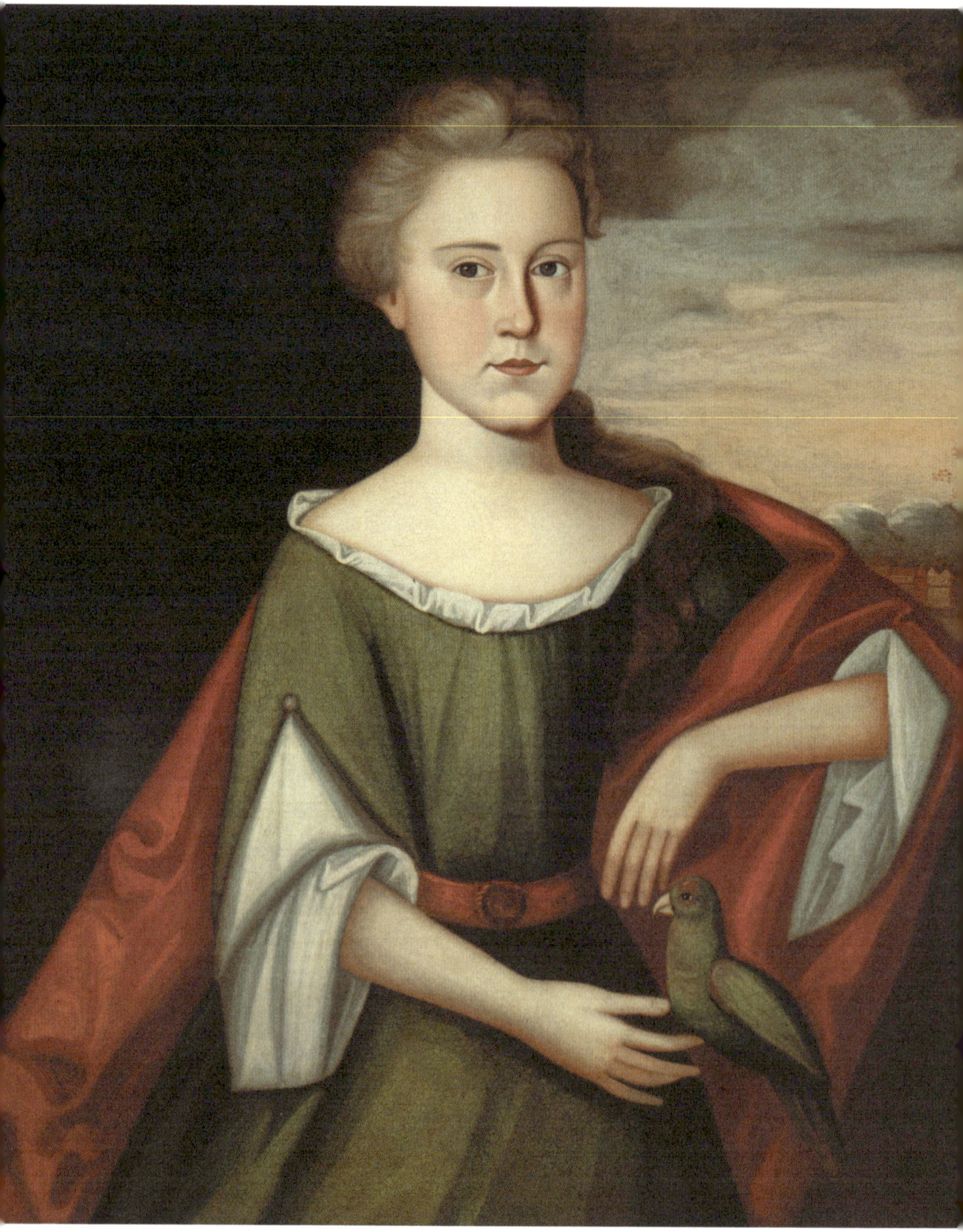

## Dorothy Quincy

CIRCA 1720    Portrait by an unidentified artist.
Bequest of Oliver Wendell Holmes, Jr., 1936.

> *Lips that lover has never kissed;*
> *Taper fingers and slender wrist;*
> *Hanging sleeves of stiff brocade;*
> *So they painted the little maid.*

Physician and poet Oliver Wendell Holmes was so taken with this portrait of his great-grandmother as "a young girl in antique costume, which made her look at first sight almost like a grown woman," that he wrote a poem dedicated to it, "Dorothy Q: A Family Portrait."

*following pages*

## Phillis Wheatley

1773    Poems on Various Subjects, Religious and Moral.
Bequest of Robert Cassie Waterston, 1899.

Phillis Wheatley was eight or nine years old in 1761 when she arrived in Boston on the slave ship *Phillis* and was sold to the Wheatley family. She became an accomplished poet and traveled to London, where her poems were first published in 1773. She was freed the same year, but her early success waned and she died in obscurity and poverty in 1784. The Historical Society holds approximately one half of her few surviving manuscripts.

PHILLIS WHEATLEY, NEGRO SERVANT to M.<sup>r</sup> JOHN WHEATLEY, of BOSTON.

Published according to Act of Parliament, Sept.<sup>r</sup> 1, 1773 by Arch.<sup>d</sup> Bell, Bookseller N.<sup>o</sup> 8 near the Saracens Head Aldgate.

# POEMS

## ON

## VARIOUS SUBJECTS,

### RELIGIOUS AND MORAL.

#### BY

#### PHILLIS WHEATLEY,

NEGRO SERVANT to Mr. JOHN WHEATLEY, of BOSTON, in NEW ENGLAND.

---

LONDON:
Printed for A. BELL, Bookseller, Aldgate; and sold by Messrs. COX and BERRY, King-Street, BOSTON.

MDCCLXXIII.

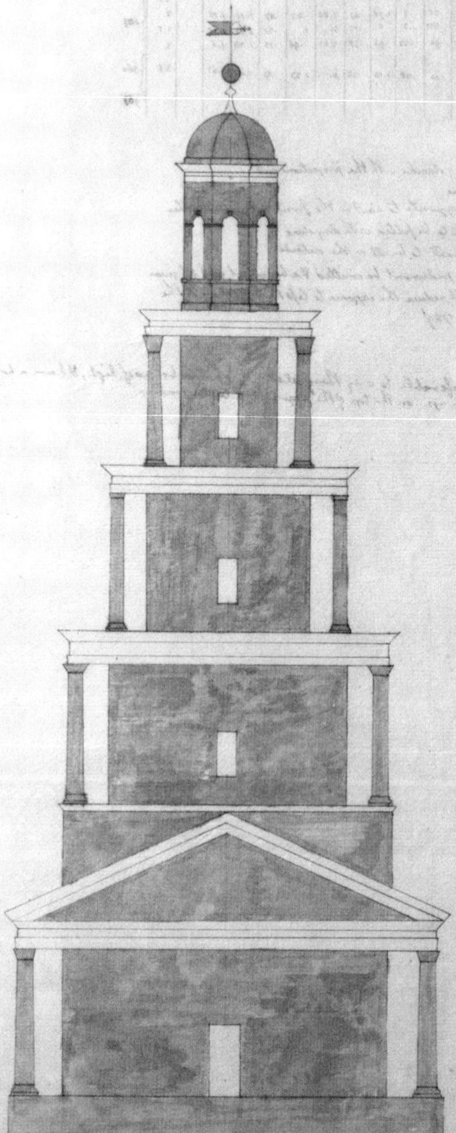

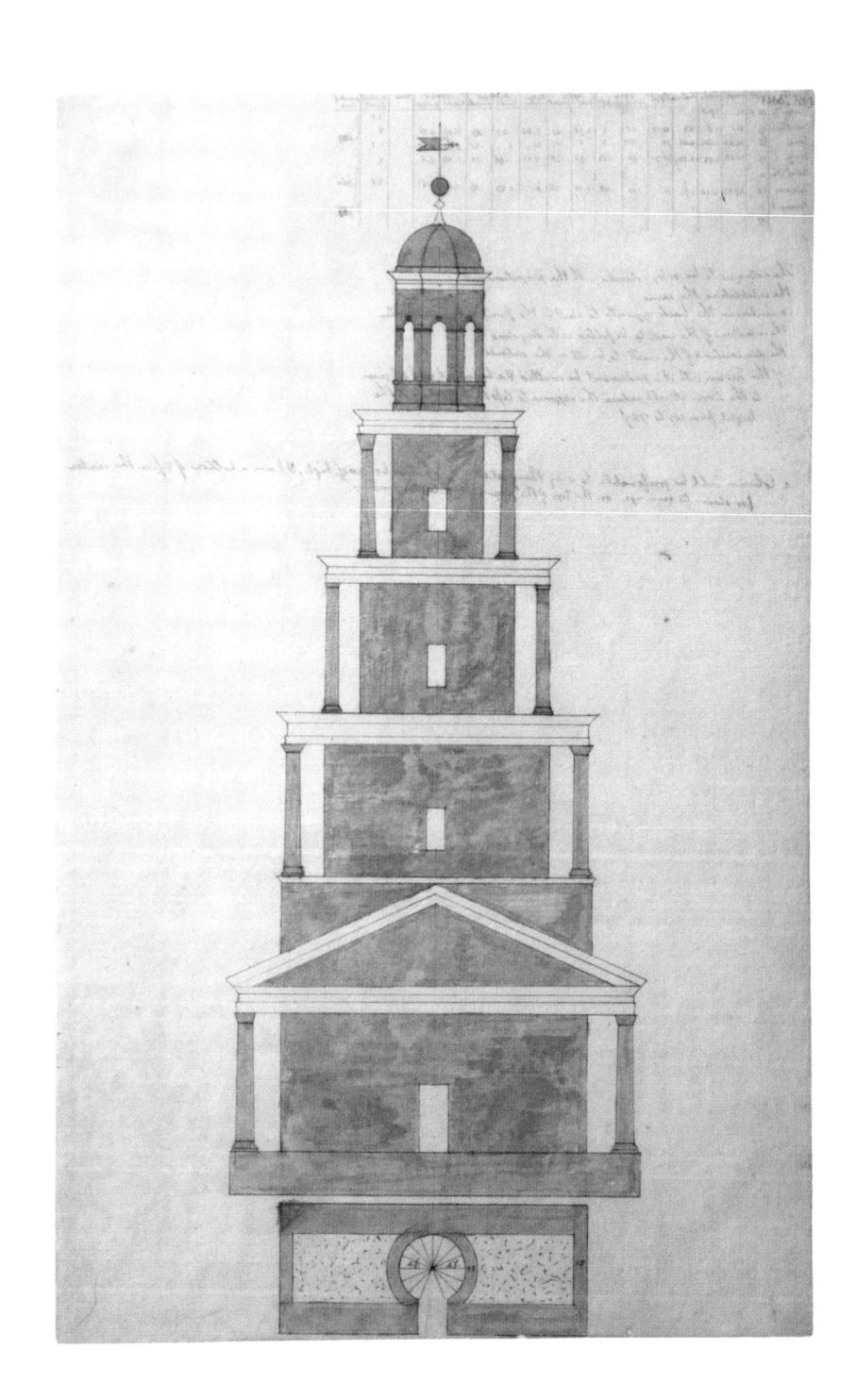

## Thomas Jefferson ~ Monticello

**CIRCA 1771**   Plan of an observation tower.
Gift of Thomas Jefferson Coolidge, Jr., 1911.

"Architecture is my delight, and putting up and pulling down one of my favorite amusements," wrote Thomas Jefferson. Never was that more true than of his beloved home, Monticello, which he first started planning when he was twenty-four. Of more than 400 architectural drawings in the Coolidge Collection of Thomas Jefferson Manuscripts in the Historical Society, half pertain to Monticello. They bear witness to Jefferson's exquisite attention to details large and small. During his diplomatic career in Europe in the 1780s, Jefferson became a disciple of Palladio, who influenced Jefferson throughout the remainder of his life as he designed his home, the Virginia Capitol at Richmond, and the University of Virginia campus, which he considered his architectural masterpiece.

*following pages*

## Thomas Jefferson ~ Monticello

**CIRCA 1771**   Final elevation of the first version.
Gift of Thomas Jefferson Coolidge, Jr., 1911.

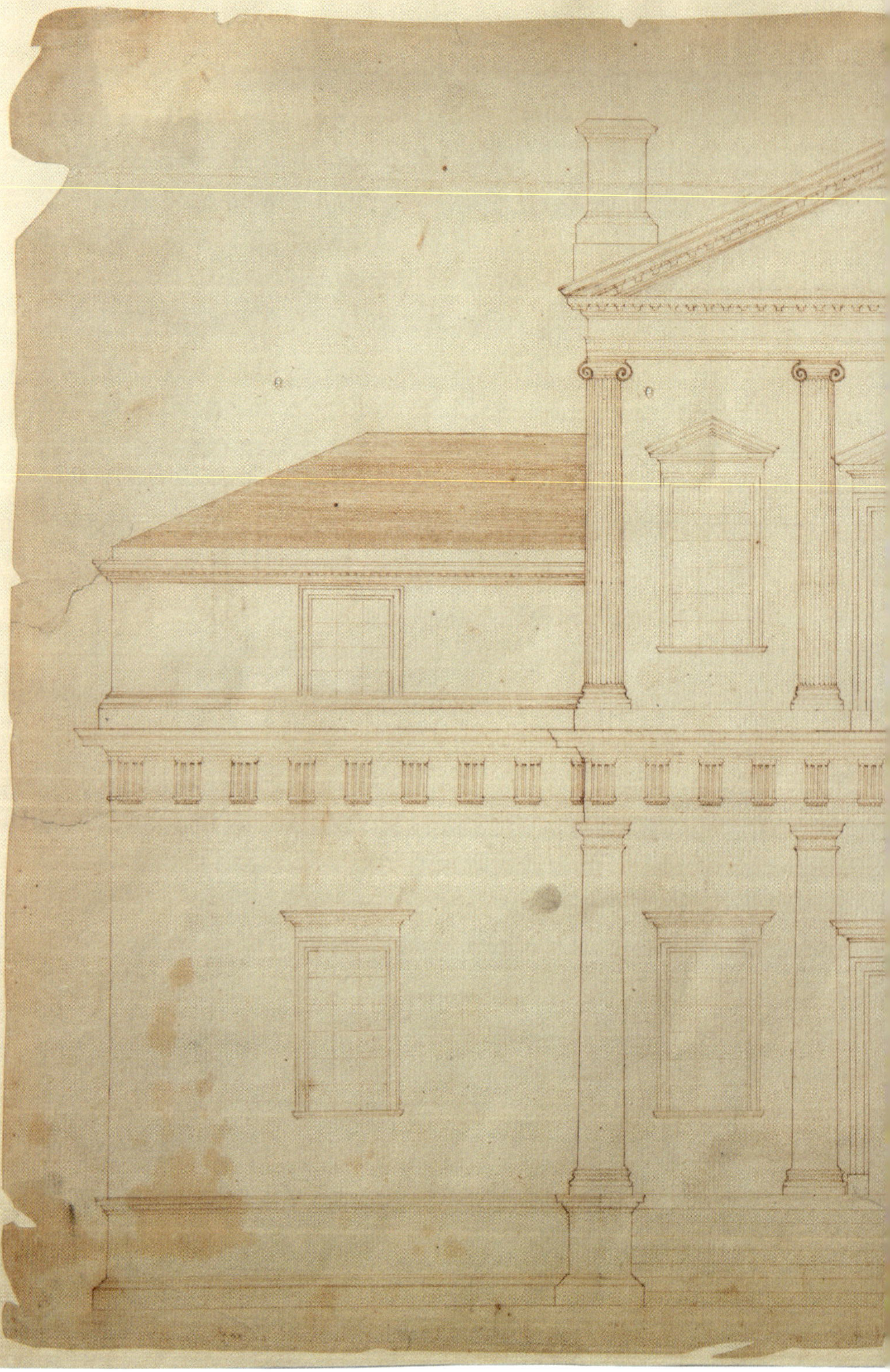

K 2 3
N 48

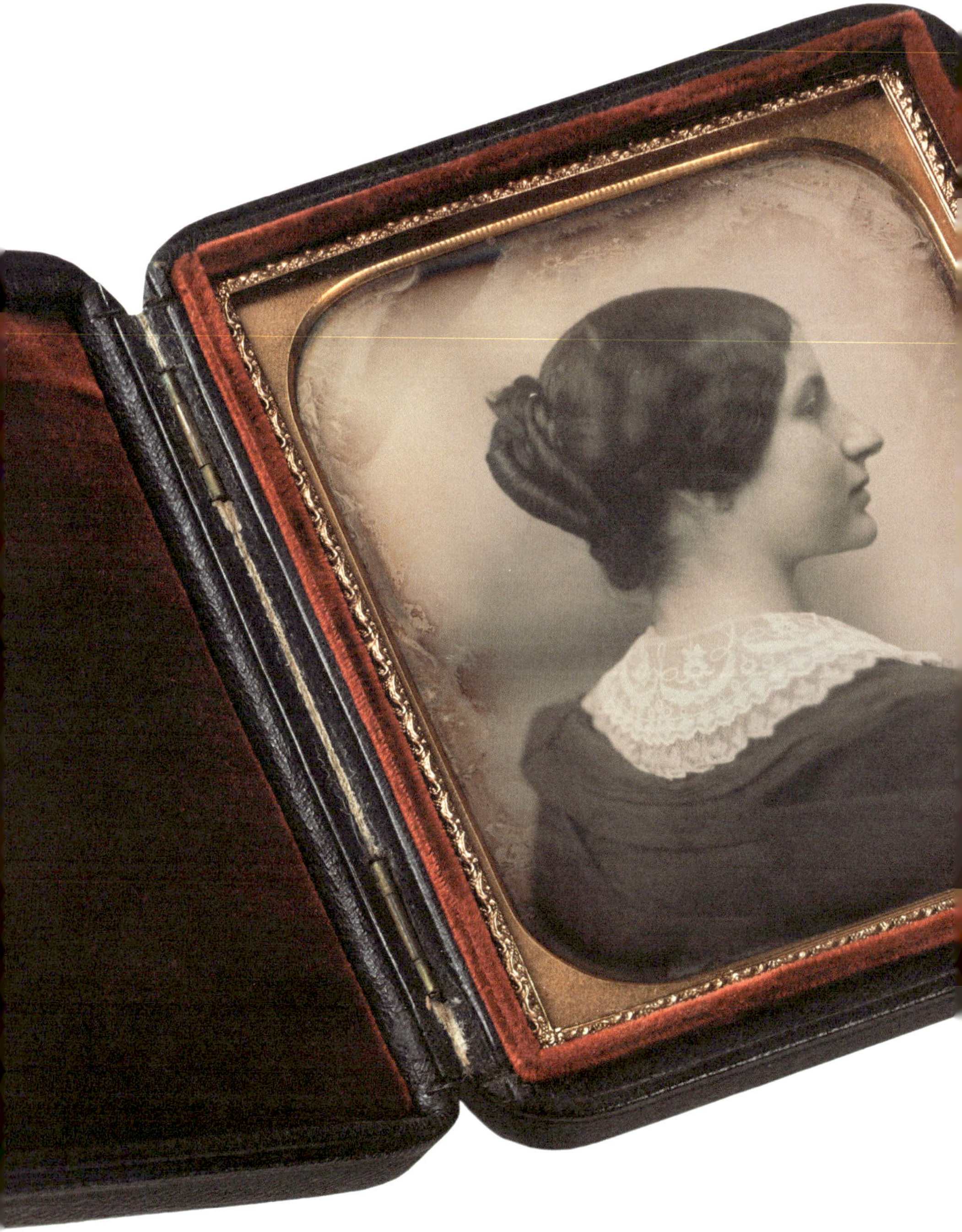

## Albert S. Southworth and Josiah J. Hawes ~ Annie Adams Fields

1853   Gift of Boylston Beale, 1941.

Photographed a year before her marriage to publisher James T. Fields in 1854, Annie Adams Fields was an author and social reformer who made her home the center of literary Boston. The Fields' circle of friends included authors published by her husband in the *Atlantic Monthly*, as well as European writers who visited Boston. In addition to her role as a literary hostess, Fields wrote biographical sketches and edited the letters of Harriet Beecher Stowe, Sarah Orne Jewett, and Celia Thaxter. The Historical Society holds her correspondence with English and American writers, and seventy volumes of her diaries and travel journals.

I wrote my journal, and
's. When I came home
evening Nelly Gordon ca
us.

g I played with Hele
front of our house, a
d time. In the eve
nd Mary u
school I studie

school 5 9 I called for
uld not come, because
dancing school

## Sarah Gooll Putnam ~ Diary entry
21 JANUARY 1861   Gift of Mrs. Sarah Buckminster Hayden, 1964.

Sarah Gooll Putnam, a Boston portrait artist, began her diary on Thanksgiving Day in 1860 when she was nine years old. Putnam continued her diary until her death in 1912, filling twenty-seven volumes. The diaries are richly illustrated with approximately 400 watercolor paintings and chronicle Putnam's career as an artist as well as her extensive travels throughout the United States and abroad.

There are more than 2,000 separate diaries in the Historical Society's manuscript collection, diaries that record, through the personal observations of events, the entire course of American history. There are journals kept by famous historical figures, beginning with John Winthrop's account of the founding of Massachusetts, but the strength of the collection lies in accounts of everyday life and the personal reflections of ordinary men, women, and children.

*following pages*

## Sarah Gooll Putnam ~ Diary entries
29 NOVEMBER ~ 3 DECEMBER 1861
Gift of Mrs. Sarah Buckminster Hayden, 1964.

November.

afternoon I played cards with Helen Paine; she lives, or rather boards in Bowdoin street.

Friday 29th In the morning when I went to school it was pretty snowy, and in the afternoon I did not do much, but look at Hatty make some dancing books May is now painting with some oil colors, and is paiting a picture, which she is going to give to Grand mother, when it is done.

Saturday 30th In the morning when I looked out of my window I thought the snow looked dry, but when I was was going to school it was so sloshy that I got my feet all wet, so that I asked Miss Demond (My teacher) if I could stand before the fire, and of course she let me, with some other girls, that were wet too. I did not go out in the afternoon. Hatty, and Mary are going to the dancing school every Thursday.

December.

Sunday 1st of December. Christmas is coming nearer, nearer!, and when it is come we shall go to cousin Jane Gray's again, and then for the weeks vacation! we shall have fun, I am going to give a good many presents, one thing I should like to have for a present would be a dictionary, and another would be a box of oil water color paints, so that I could paint pictures that looked like oil color paint, and I could paint things nicely with such paints, as the paints that I have now are oly water colors. As there are so many union pictures in the newspapers that I thought I would paste one in here. In the morning Mother and Hatty went to church, and Johnny, and at home, and read. At about I stayed twelve oclock I took a walk with Mary, and Johnny down Beacon street.

Monday 2nd In the afternoon I stayed at home, and did not do much.

Tuesday 3rd In the Imorning I went with Mother to Dr Clarks to have my ear fixed, and Mother, and I had to wait a quater of an houre, before he came.

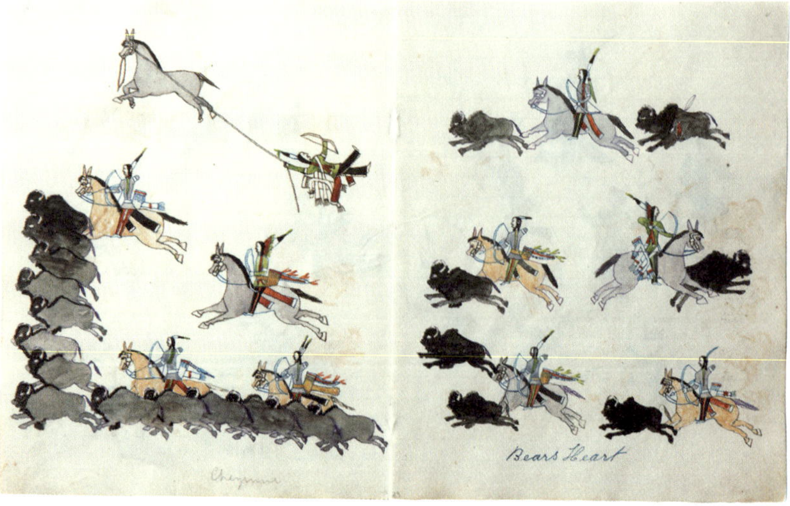
Cheyenne
Bears Heart

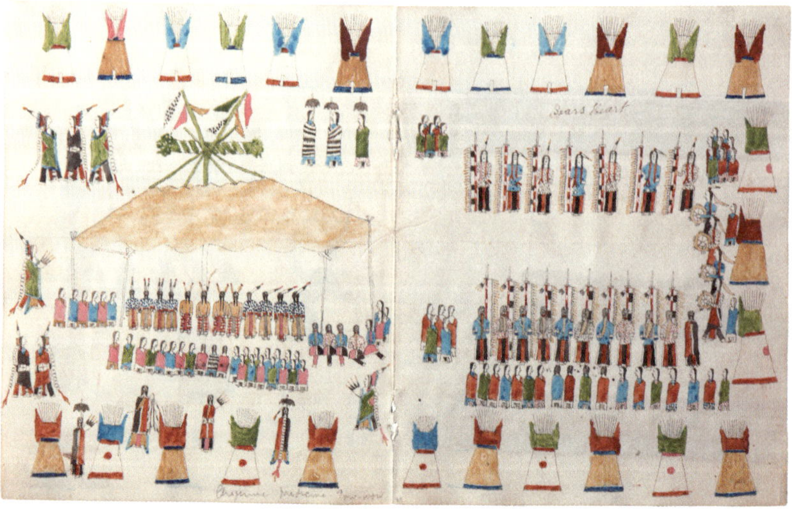
Bears Heart

## Bear's Heart ~ Buffalo Hunt

CIRCA 1876-1877   From Book of Sketches made at Fort Marion, St. Augustine, Florida. Gift of Mrs. John Forbes Perkins, 1956.

These colorful drawings, created by a Cheyenne warrior during his imprisonment in Florida after the Red River War in 1874–1875, derive from traditional Native American art and are examples of ledger art—named for the bound volumes provided by their warders in which the artists recorded camp life, hunts, and battles, as well as scenes of their imprisonment.

This volume came to Massachusetts from Florida as a token of thanks for the kindness shown to Howling Wolf, another Cheyenne captive, who came to Boston for an eye operation during his imprisonment.

## Bear's Heart ~ Cheyenne Medicine Pow-wow

CIRCA 1876-1877   From Book of Sketches made at Fort Marion, St. Augustine, Florida. Gift of Mrs. John Forbes Perkins, 1956.

### John Singer Sargent ~ Peter Chardon Brooks III
1890   Gift of Mrs. Levin H. Campbell and George Lewis, 2004.

John Singer Sargent was at the height of his powers when he painted this portrait of Peter Chardon Brooks III in 1890. Brooks had inherited part of the fortune of his grandfather, the Boston merchant and philanthropist Peter Chardon Brooks, and put his money to work developing Chicago real estate. In 1881, he commissioned architects Burnham & Root to design the Montauk Block, Chicago's first skyscraper. When the firm completed the taller Monadnock Building for him in 1891, it was the largest office building in the world.

The marriage of Peter Chardon Brooks III to Sarah Lawrence, the daughter of Amos Adams Lawrence, united two families long settled in New England. The marriage of their daughter, Eleanor Brooks, to Richard Middlecott Saltonstall connected the Lawrence, Brooks, and Saltonstall families—all represented in large collections of personal papers, photographs, and portraits held by the Historical Society.

# About the Massachusetts Historical Society

The goal of the Historical Society's founders was "to collect, preserve and communicate materials for a complete history of this country." More than 215 years after its founding, the MHS remains faithful to its mission and at the forefront of its field.

The Massachusetts Historical Society

- provides unparalleled resources to thousands of researchers each year;

- encourages new historical scholarship through fellowships, seminars, and conferences;

- offers an extensive program of fellowships and workshops for teachers;

- publishes a range of printed and digital resources—including documentary editions, essay collections, and an annual journal;

- produces the *Adams Papers*, an authoritative edition of the correspondence, diaries, and family papers of Presidents John and John Quincy Adams;

- expands the impact of its collections through the online display of primary sources;

- sponsors an array of engaging public programs—including lectures, booksignings, and discussion series; and

- presents public exhibitions of materials from its collections and tours of its national historic landmark building.

To learn more about the Historical Society's programs and services, visit our website at www.masshist.org.

For more information on the items featured in this book, visit www.masshist.org/gallery.